The west side of Caverswall Castle

THE CASTLES AND MOATED MANSIONS OF STAFFORDSHIRE AND THE WEST MIDLANDS COUNTY

CONTENTS

A GLOSSARY OF TERMS

Ashlar - Masonry of blocks with even faces and square edges.
Barbican - Porch, tower, or enclosure defending a gateway.
Batter - The inward inclination of a wall face.
Battlement - A parapet with crenellations protecting a wallwalk.
Chamfer - A slope made by cutting off a right angled edge.
Chancel - The eastern part of a church containing the altar.
Crenellations - Indentations in a parapet.
Curtain Walls - High stone walls around a castle bailey.
Jamb - the side of a doorway, window, or other opening.
Keep - A building or small court acting as a citadel.
Light - A compartment of a window.
Lintel - A horizontal stone or bean spanning an opening.
Machicolation - Slots behind a parapet for dropping missiles.
Merlons - The upstanding portions of a crenellated parapet.
Moat - A ditch, wet or dry, around an enclosure.
Motte - Steep mound, usually at least partly artificial.
Mullion - A vertical member dividing the lights of a window.
Plinth - The projecting base of a wall, often battered.
Portcullis - Gate designed to rise and fall in vertical grooves.
Postern - A secondary gateway or back doorway.
Quoins - Dressed stones at the corners of a building.
Shell Keep - Small stone walled enclosure on top of a motte.
Solar - Castle owner's living room, often also his bedroom.
Transom - Horizontal member dividing to & bottom window lights.
Wall Walk - A walkway on a wall top, protected by a parapet.

SUMMARY OF REFERENCES

The History and Antiquities of Staffordshire, Stebbing Shaw, 1798
The Buildings of Staffordshire, Nikolaus Pevsner, 1974
The Buildings of Warwickshire, Nikolaus Pevsner, 1966
A History of Staffordshire, M.W.Greenslade & D.G.Stuart, 1965
The Victoria County History of Staffordshire, several vols
The Victoria County History of Warwickshire, several vols
Norman Castles in Britain, Derek Renn, 1968
Medieval Newcastle-Under-Lyme, T.Pape, 1928
Transactions of the North Staffordshire Field Club
Transactions of the South Staffordshire Archeological & Historical Society
Transactions of the Birmingham and The West Midlands Archeological Society
Medieval Archeology
Country Life
William Salt Archeological Society Annual transactions
Biddulph Historical Society Publications

HISTORICAL AND ARCHITECTURAL INTRODUCTION

THE EARLIEST CASTLES

This book is essentially about medieval buildings which illustrate the old saying that an Englishman's home is his castle. Those here described either had a genuine dual purpose as both fortress and private residence, or were basically domestic buildings which were given features traditionally associated with fortifications to show the rank, prestige, and power of the owner.

The concept of a privately owned fortress cum residence was little known in England prior to the invasion of William, Duke of Normandy, in 1066. He established here the feudal system in which lords held numerous units of land called manors directly from the King in return for military service, and then gave many of their manors to knights and lesser lords on the same basis. The veneer of French speaking Normans consolidated their hold on these lands inhabited by the Saxon populace by building themselves fortified residences which they called castles. However, some Saxons stayed in power. Edwin, Earl of Mercia, and lord of much of the area we are considering, did not oppose William in 1066, and his Earldom was only abolished when he rebelled and was defeated and killed in 1071. A Saxon called Richard Chenvin was appointed as custodian of the royal forest of Cannock, a prestigious and important office, and families such as the Bagots are said to be of Saxon, rather than Norman, origin.

King William came to the midlands in 1069 and 1070 to put down rebellions, and on the latter occasion he had a castle built beside the town of Stafford. This has now vanished, but analogy with the contemporary castles at Warwick and Shrewsbury suggests it was of earth and wood rather than stone. A circular ditch would have been dug and the materials piled in the middle to make a mound or motte on which was built a timber house or tower set within a stockade. On one side would have been a palisade and ditch enclosing a court or bailey containing scattered wooden buildings serving as a hall, chapel, stables, barns, granary, workshops, and so on.

When the Earldom of Mercia was abolished King William gave a large estate west of Stafford to his hereditary standard bearer Roger de Toeni, whose son Robert took the surname de Stafford and founded the noble family of that name, destined to become Dukes of Buckingham. At the time of the Domesday survey of 1086 Robert de Stafford was the chief landholder in Staffordshire after the King. It was probably soon afterwards that he raised the fine motte and bailey castle 2km west of Stafford as his fortress, administrative centre, and chief residence. At this time the Earl of Shrewsbury held much land in Staffordshire, although his castles were mostly in Shropshire, while Henry de Ferrers held a large estate in NE Staffordshire, and Derbyshire, centered on a castle at Tutbury, and William Fitz-Ansculf held what is now called the Black Country, plus Walsall, with a castle at Dudley. Robert Marmion constructed the castle at Tamworth, and by the turn of the century the Earl of Chester had a large Warwickshire estate with a castle at Coventry, and a Staffordshire estate centered on a castle at Chartley. These castles were of the type described above, adapted according to the terrain and resources available. Most had one or two outer baileys in addition to the basic motte and bailey plan. The other castles of this type in the area may date from the 12th century. Newcastle -under-Lyme and Castle Bromwich each had a mound and single bailey, while at Audley, Biddulph, and perhaps Ashley, natural hills were shaped into large low mounds without adjoining baileys.

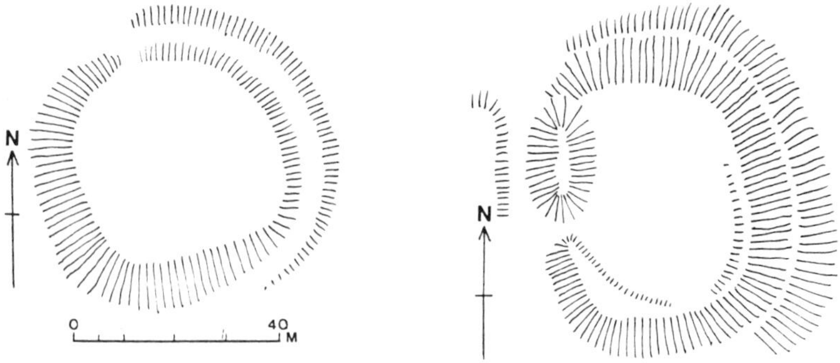

PLANS OF AUDLEY MOTTE (left) & BIDDULPH MOTTE (right)

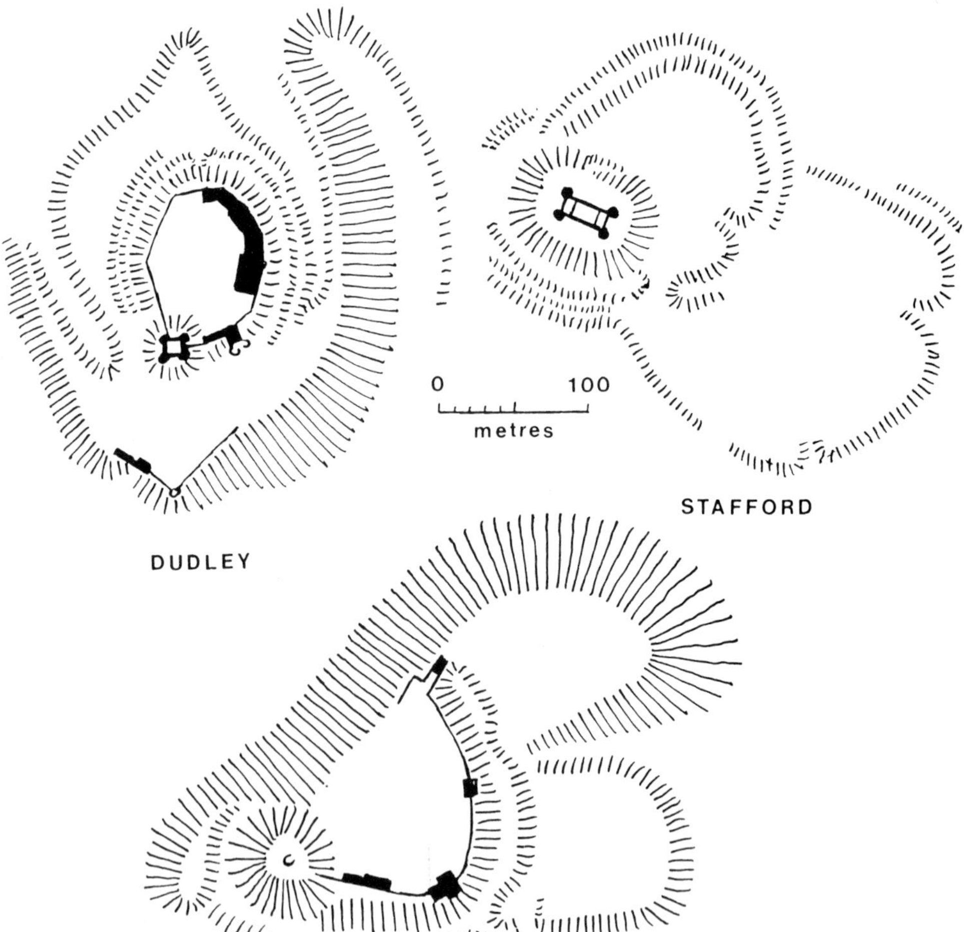

PLANS OF MOTTE AND BAILEY CASTLES IN STAFFORDSHIRE

Tutbury Castle: The Motte

Contemporary chronicles and documents show that castles played a very important part in the conflicts between King Stephen (1135-54) and the supporters of Henry I's daughter Matilda, who included the Earl of Chester, and the Paganels, now lords of Dudley. Their castles saw much action (see p48 and p50). On the other hand Robert de Ferrers of Tutbury was made earl of Derby in 1138 for supporting King Stephen at the battle of Northallerton.

THE FIRST STONE CASTLES

Timber is vulnerable to accidental or deliberate destruction by fire, and soon rots away when in constant contact with the soil. Gradually timber structures were rebuilt in mortared stone. In the area under discussion the only surviving stonework earlier than c1170 is at Tamworth. The wall bearing the pathway up the mound is faced with herringbone masonry which must be of c1100-50 and the shell keep, a thick stone substitute for the original palisade on the edge of the mound summit, may only be a little later. Within it would have once been lean-to timber buildings replacing the original freestanding wooden house or tower. Some of the functions of the latter may have been taken over by the contemporary square tower projecting slightly from the shell towards the approach.

On his accession in 1154 Henry II began to restore the balance between royal castles and baronial ones by a policy of keeping some confiscated castles in his own hands, building new ones, and having those belonging to barons of dubious loyalty demolished. Probably it was he who had built a rectangular stone tower keep at Newcastle-under-Lyme. Like the keep he built at Bridgnorth in the 1160s it would have had pilaster buttresses on the corners and an entrance above ground level leading into the living room or hall. A spiral stair in a corner by the entrance would have led down to a dark cellar, and up to a private room and the battlements. It has gone, but a few courses remain of what was probably a smaller copy of it built on one side of the mound summit at Stafford Castle.

The rebellion led by the King's sons in 1173-4 gave Henry II a new opportunity to destroy the castles of rebel barons, including those of Tutbury and Dudley, and repossession was only allowed on payment of a heavy fine. Tutbury was soon rebuilt and certainly had a stone chapel by the 1190s, and probably also a shell keep. The de Verduns' built a stone castle at Alton in this era and the castle at Coventry may have had stone buildings of this period, but the 12th century buildings at Weoley, Richard I's hunting lodge at Stourton, and Eccleshall Castle were still of earth and timber.

The basement of the Gateway at Tamworth Castle

LATER STONE CASTLES

From his succession as Earl of Chester in 1180 until his death in 1232, Ranulph de Blundeville was one of the most powerful men of his time. For loyalty to the Crown in the troubled period 1214-18 he was entrusted with the keeping of Newcastle under Lyme and also Peveril Castle in Derbyshire in 1215, had possession of Lancashire from 1216, and in 1217 gained the Earldom of Lincoln. He was on a crusade in the Holy Land from May 1218 until August 1220, and it was on his return, no doubt inspired by more advanced stronghold designs there, that he began three remarkable castles at Beeston in Cheshire, Bolingbroke in Lincolnshire, and Chartley in Stafford--shire. At Chartley he built on the older mound a large round tower keep with a round projecting stair turret facing towards the inner bailey, which was given stone walls flanked by five large circular three storey towers. Two of the towers were set either side of the gateway, and all of them had crossloops for discharging crossbows.

Heighley Castle was built by Henry de Audley, probably in the 1220s. De Audley was an associate of Earl Ranulph and Heighley is similar to Beeston Castle in its spectacular setting. It is very ruined, but analogy with Ranulph's three new castles, and limited evidence on site, suggests that it had two large D-shaped towers flanking the gateway. Nothing now remains visible of a third castle of this era with round flanking towers, built at Stourton by Henry III's forester of Kinver. In 1260 a bailey gateway was built at Tamworth with shallow round projections set either side of the entrance passageway, below which was a basement which is now all that survives.

Weoley Castle: The west side.

Caverswall Castle: The Gateway

By the reign of King John (1199-1216) the building of embattled (crenellated) walls and towers had to be authorised by the Crown. Licences to crenellate were only granted to a loyal privileged few so that defensive features became a sign of high rank and privilage and were sometimes built after they ceased to have any real military function. The many surviving records of licences granted up to the early 16th century help historians to date many embattled houses. Under the terms of licences granted during the last third of the 13th century the manor houses at Weoley, Caverswall, and Eccleshall were made into castles, and an embattled wall with gatehouses and corner towers was built around the cathedral close at Lichfield. Weoley has a rather irregular plan with a comparatively thin outer wall with several square towers, one of which was the gatehouse. Caverswall and Eccleshall were more regular rectangles with walls about 2m thick rising directly from the bottom of the former wet moats, and flanked by polygonal corner towers, with two more such towers flanking the gateway in the middle of one side, as at many of the much stronger castles of this period in North Wales. All four enclosures are low lying with defences only really adequate against minor local unrest and were built when this area enjoyed peace and prosperity under Edward I.

Of the same period is the Butlers' mansion at Norbury, where there were probably four ranges set around an open court within a wet moat. It was probably never embattled and without towers save for a bartizan of aesthetic rather than military purpose at one corner. It was one of the earliest of many medieval mansions with outer walls only a metre or so thick where the provision of a moat crossed only by a drawbridge, and the fixing of iron grilles or bars on any outer windows within easy reach, was deemed adequate to keep out undesirables. The manor houses which were licensed to be crenellated in the 14th century at Bescot, Caludon, Langley, Madeley, and Walsall would have been similar either to Caverswall or Norbury, while that at Swynnerton may never have been built. It is also uncertain what, if anything, was built at Wolseley, after a licence to crenellate was granted in 1469.

Tutbury Castle: The North Tower.

Tutbury Castle: The South Towe

The tower houses built upon the mound summits at Dudley and Stafford are of particular interest in that new castles of their era usually took the quadrangular open court with corner towers plan of Caverswall and Eccleshall and, more completely preserved, Maxstoke Castle in Warwickshire. The tower at Dudley was probably built by Sir John de Somery in c1305-20. It was accompanied by a bailey wall with a gatehouse but without the flanking towers often provided in this period, military strength being concentrated on the single huge tower designed as the lord's personal residence. He is described as a difficult and domineering neighbour, and his tower was evidently designed as a sign of dominance over both his tenants and neighbours. It has four large circular corner towers, producing a plan found in a small number of keeps in France and Ireland, and in England at the small mid 13th century Ypres Tower at Rye, and at the keep of Mulgrave Castle, North Yorkshire, as rebuilt in c1300-10. However, the corner towers at Dudley are of less projection than the other examples, and internally were closed off only by wooden partitions, so the mid 13th century quatrefoil lobed keeps at York and Pontefract could also possibly be regarded as models for the tower's rather individual layout and design.

Lord Stafford's tower of c1347-60 at Stafford owes something to Dudley, but because of its greater length was more like a manor house with octagonal corner towers. It contained considerably more accommodation than the tower at Dudley. It had predecessors in the two storey hall houses with corner turrets built at Tarset and Edlingham in Northumberland in the late 13th century, but must also have been inspired by buildings Lord Stafford saw in France during his long years of military service there. The machicolated parapet stipulated for it in the building contract of 1347 would have been one of the earliest examples of this form of defence in Britain.

The gatehouse which Thomas, Earl of Lancaster built at Tutbury as part of a general remodelling of the castle is rather modest compared with many contemporary gatehouses, especially that which he built at Dunstanburgh. However, more exciting things were to come at Tutbury, for most of the curtain walls were built anew in the first half of the 15th century, together with two self contained tower houses. This work, begun for Henry IV, and continued by Henry VI and his Queen, Margaret of Anjou, has few parallels. It was rare for a much older castle to have its defences so extensively renewed in that era, when work was usually confined to repairs, and some improvements to the domestic buildings. The tower houses, combining the provision of secure and very private lordly accommodation with the needs of defence, are predecessors of several great towers, built as refuges and status symbols by Edward IV and his leading supporters in the 1470s. The tower of c1500 at Hamstall Ridware is a much humbler echo of these, usable only as a lookout point.

MOATED SITES

Scattered across England are moated enclosures marking the sites of former manor houses. Excavations may reveal that some once had stone walls like at Norbury, but many only had a hedge or fence on the inner side of the moat with a timber framed house inside. Some have been superseded by farmhouses of the 16th century and later built of more durable materials either within the moated platform or just outside it.

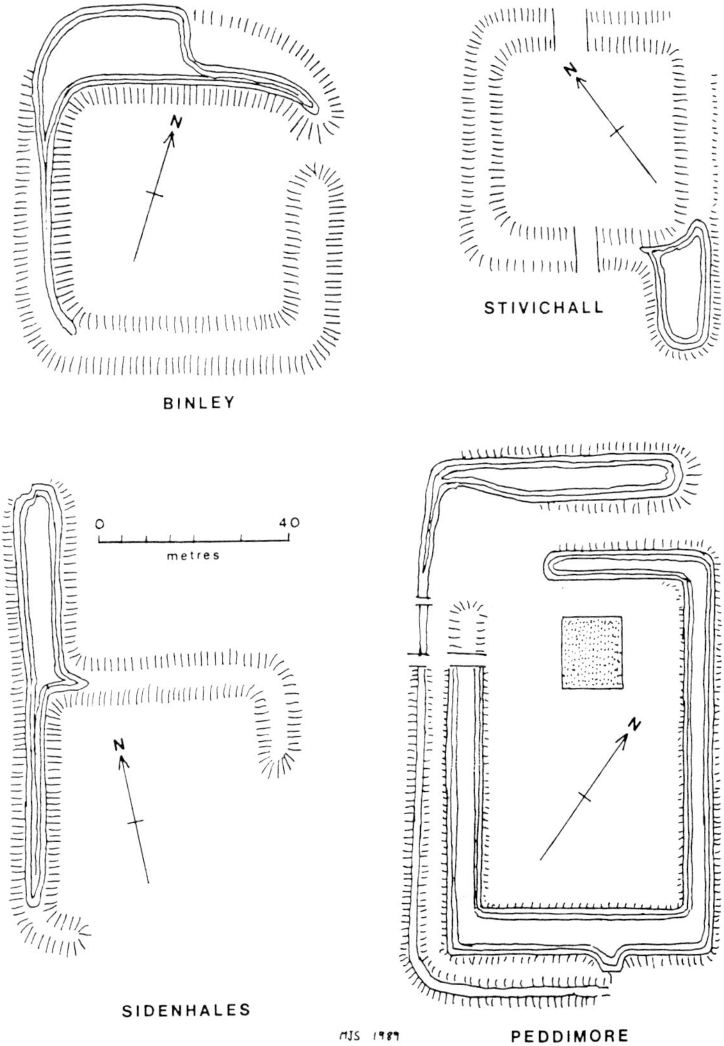

PLANS OF MOATED SITES IN THE WEST MIDLANDS COUNTY

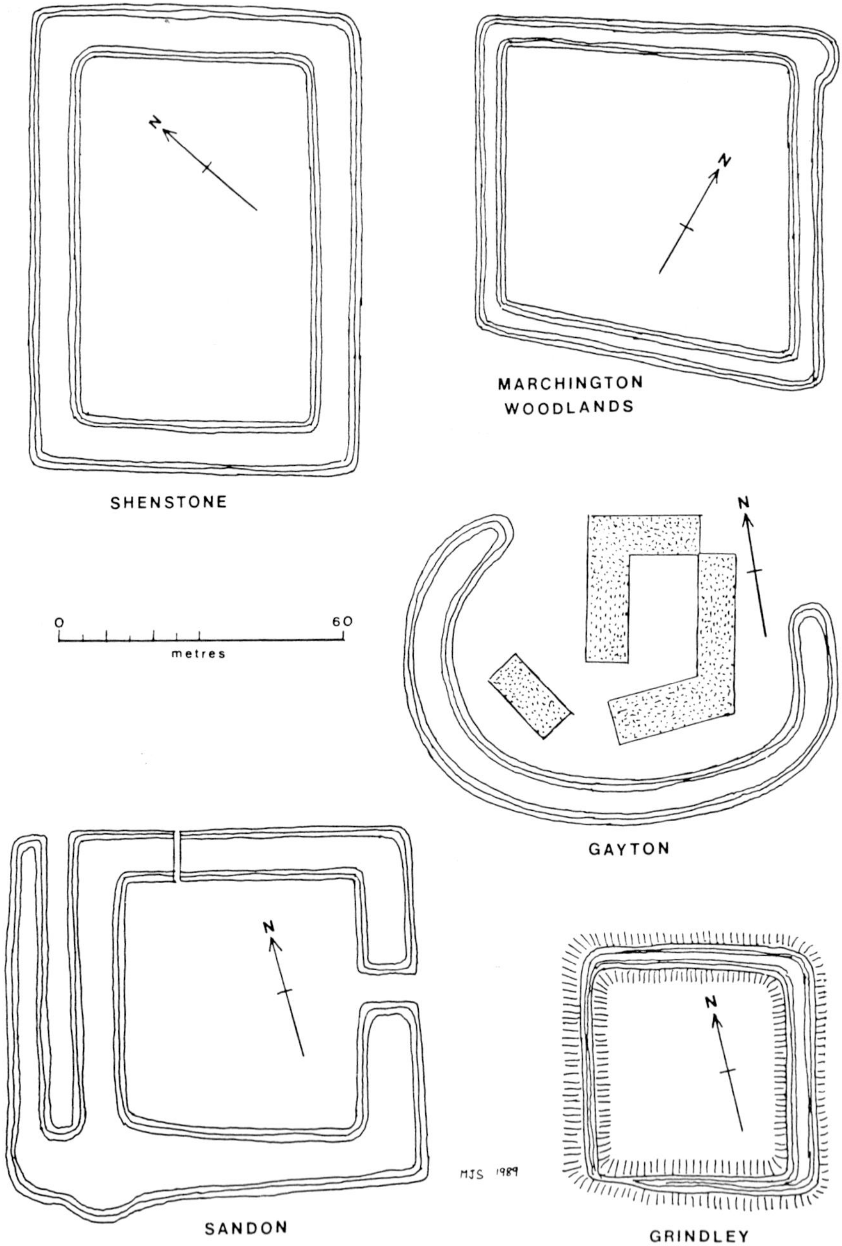

PLANS OF MOATED SITES IN STAFFORDSHIRE

A dry moat in a field close to The Abnalls, near Lichfield

Several excavations and much research have been done on moated sites in the West Midlands County and southern Staffordshire in the last 25 years, but some questions remain unanswered. Some moats are of the 12th century, but the majority date from the 13th and 14th centuries, and it has been suggested that several were constructed in response to the periods of unrest in the reigns of Henry III and Edward II. Quite a number appear to have been disused after c1400, but a few fresh moats were dug in the 15th century, and at Tamworth and Wolverhampton were 16th century town houses with, as far as we know, freshly dug moats of that period. Moated sites often occur in groups of two or three because of manors being split between heiresses, or a simple abandonment of a site and the creation of a new one. Some moats were only occupied for a generation or two but others have never been vacant since first created.

A water filled ditch around a manor house was not necessarily military in purpose. A moat is quite a permanent and efficient boundary for keeping vagrants, wild animals, and malefactors out, and domestic animals, servants, and children in. At all periods moats have been appreciated as scenic features, and they served as a habitat for fish, eels, and water fowl, which together formed a substantial part of the medieval diet. A wet moat could also help to drain land otherwise unsuitable for inhabitation or agriculture, and could be used as a source of water for cooking, brewing, and washing. Because of these many uses to which they were put, moats did not require royal consent of the sort required for embattled walls and towers, but they still had some function as symbols of status as only the lords of manors and some of the more wealthy of the parochial clergy had the land and wealth needed to create them.

The words motte and moat are clearly related. Although modern historians understand them to mean different types of earthworks, this was not the case in the medieval period. A dwelling referred to as being on a "mote" or "motte" in a 14th century document may have been either upon an 11th or 12th century castle mound of the usual upturned pudding bowl shape, or set on flat ground or a low platform surrounded by a water filled ditch of more recent origin. Naturally the former might be regarded as more defensible, but this is often not made clear in old records. One might expect a gradual development from high conical mounds to low rectangular platforms.

The low round mound at Weston Jones, and the unusually small square platforms which rise above the ground outside the moats at Ribden and Burnhill Green, may perhaps be a transitional type between the motte and the common rectangular moated platforms with sides about 30m to 60m long only rising slightly, if at all, above the ground level outside the moat. Round enclosures with platforms level with the ground outside are uncommon, but they occur in Staffordshire at Gayton and Coppenhall Gorse. Excavation has shown that the latter was occupied in the 14th century. Several sites changed shape when rebuilt in later centuries, both Weoley and Eccleshall having more rounded enclosures in c1200 before being rebuilt in stone. The irregularly shaped moat and ramparts at Chiswick Green were shown to have been created in c1300 at a previously unenclosed site. At Blithewood and Peddimore there were concentric outer moats and a number of sites have additional enclosures and/or fishponds.

DOMESTIC BUILDINGS AT THE CASTLES

Not much has survived of the domestic buildings of the castles and fortified manor houses, which were more lightly constructed than the defences. From the medieval period there survives only a block which contained the solar and chapel at Dudley, foundations of a fairly full set of buildings at Weoley, part of the hall at Caludon and the base of the chapel at Tutbury. The remains at Weoley are interesting as they can be compared with a detailed 15th century account of the castle, and their uses identified. They follow the usual layout with a hall with a solar at one end, and a kitchen at the other, set on the opposite side of the courtyard from the gate.

Until the Tudor period glass was uncommon in secular buildings and windows would have been closed with shutters, while furnishings would also have been sparse, especially when the lord was absent. In order to consume agricultural produce and administer their many manors on the spot, great lords tended to circulate from one castle or manor house to another, taking their servants and transportable furnishings with them, and leaving only caretakers behind at each.

THE TUDOR AND STUART PERIODS

Cannon began to make high walls and towers militarily redundant during the late 15th century. With just one possible exception of some bastions that may have been built at Burton in the 1540s, no military structures were built within the area under discussion between 1460 and the Civil War. Domestic buildings continued to be added, the hall of c1450-1500 in the keep at Tamworth, and the splendid apartments of c1550 at Dudley being the most notable, and in the early 17th century considerable work was done at Caverswall and Tamworth. Documentation is much fuller for this period, giving us quite a lot of information about destroyed buildings and their contents. The antiquary John Leland's comments are very useful.

Little needs to be said about the involvement of the buildings in national history between the 1450s and the 1640s. Coventry was involved in the struggles between the houses of Lancaster and York but the castles took no notable part. Dudley came to prominence in the mid 16th century as the principal seat of John Dudley, Duke of Northumberland, who had the temerity to try and crown his daughter -in-law Lady Jane Grey as Queen in preference to Henry VIII's elder daughter Mary, and Tutbury Castle and Chartley Hall were two of the places used for the long imprisonment of Mary, Queen of scots.

THE CIVIL WAR AND AFTER

When fighting broke out between Charles I and his Parliament in 1642, many lords and gentry garrisoned and fortified their homes. A majority of them were initially held for the King, but Rushall Hall, Caverswall castle, the walled city of Coventry, and Leek and Birmingham were held for Parliament. King Charles led an abortive attack on Coventry in 1642 before the main conflict began.

In March 1643 Parliament captured Lichfield Cathedral Close, losing Lord Brooke in the process. The Royalists in turn lost a commander but gained a victory in the same month when they sallied out of Stafford to forestall a Parliamentary attack on the town, and lost the Earl of Northampton in the resulting battle of Hopton Heath. However, in May Stafford fell anyway to a surprise attack at night. Prince Rupert recaptured Lichfield Close in April and Rushall Hall, and Tamworth and Birmingham were also taken for the King, but Parliament captured Eccleshall Castle in August. Until their defeat at Nantwich early in 1644 the Royalists held the upper hand for several months in north and east Staffordshire.

In December 1643 Sir Thomas Holt garrisoned his residence at Aston Hall for the King, but it was captured just ten days later after a sharp engagement. The Earl of Denbigh recaptured Rushall Hall in May 1644, and laid siege to Dudley Castle. However he had difficulties in paying his forces and was obliged to withdraw when a royalist relief force arrived from Worcester.

In the spring of 1645 the Royalists captured Uttoxeter, Burton and Caverswall, but their defeat at Naseby in Yorkshire in June ended their hopes of victory. Their remaining garrisons were taken out one by one, although Lichfield Close held out until July 1646.

To prevent redundant strongholds being used by the Royalists, Parliament made a practice of demolishing those still fortifiable. By 1647 the shell keep at Tamworth was the only notable defensive work that had not been slighted, apart from Caverswall, which had lost much of its military value when rebuilt earlier. Eccleshall and Stourton were restored as country houses by the end of the 17th century, and in the 18th a caretakers house was put up at Tutbury. Stafford and Alton were rebuilt as residences in the 19th century although the former has become a ruin again. So, apart from the Tamworth keep, which is now a museum, the buildings described in in this book are all either very ruinous, have been altered out of recognition since the Civil War, have left behind only a moat, or have vanished altogether. *See: Greenslade & Stuart p34-7*

PUBLIC ACCESS TO THE SITES

Free access during daytime: Stafford (earthworks), Lichfield Close, Madeley, Tamworth (bailey), Caludon, Cheylesmore Manor, Audley Motte, Castle Bromwich Motte.

Fee Payable: Tamworth (keep), Tutbury, Weoley, Dudley, Blithfield

Visible from adjacent churchyards: Caverswall, Hamstall Ridware

Visible from rights of way on foot: Pillaton, Norbury, Red Moor Sinai Park, Marchington Woodlands, Hobbs Moat

Visible from public roads: Alton, Chartley, Kents Moat, Littywood, Biddulph Motte, Moats at Gayton, Knightley Dale

CASTLES AND FORTIFIED HOUSES IN STAFFORDSHIRE

ALTON CASTLE

SK 073425

This little known but spectacularly sited stronghold was built in c1170 by Bertram de Verdon. He died while on crusade with Richard I in the Holy Land in the 1190s. According to some accounts Alton Castle was ruinous at the time of Theobald de Verdun's death in 1316, when it passed by marriage to the Furnivals, but some other accounts have it that Theobald had rebuilt the castle, or perhaps more likely, its domestic buildings. By marrying the heiress Maud Furnival in 1406 John Talbot obtained Alton and the title of Lord Furnival. He probably restored the castle for occasional residence, and for his services in France was created Earl of Shrewsbury in 1442. George, 6th Earl, was husband of Bess of Hardwick and for a while had custody of Mary, Queen of Scots. Alton Castle was held for King Charles in the Civil War and was later rendered untenable by order of Parliament. in 1787 Charles Talbot, 15th Earl, began to develop an outlying lodge and its grounds on the other side of the Churnet, and the work was continued during the 19th century to create the large mansion, now ruined, called Alton Towers. In 1847 the then earl or another of the family commissioned Pugin to build a romantic mock castle on the site of the former domestic buildings of the original castle. Seven years earlier Pugin had masterminded the building of a catholic college on the other side of the moat, and the two form a remarkable group to the north of the church.

The castle lies high above the south side of the ravine of the Churnet. Pugin's building forms a roughly T-shaped plan and stands at the eastern end of an oval courtyard roughly 90m long from east to west with a maximum width of about 40m. A sheer rock face lies below the north side and a steep fall to the west. On the east and south is a sheer sided rock-cut ditch which is 18m wide by 8m deep where a modern bridge crosses it on the south. The defences must have been of masonry from the start utilising the stone taken from the ditch. The lower parts of a curtain wall about 2m thick remain around the western half of the courtyard. On the south side is a rectangular tower about 7.4m wide externally faced with ashlar. It dates from the 12th century, but the upper part, with chamfered off corners and a crossloop, and also the base of a round tower further west, are likely to be of c1300. The prominent relieving arch in the outer face of the rectangular tower is too low to be a blocked up gateway, and the castle entrance must have been further east.

See: Renn p352; Pevsner p55-60; V.C.H. Staffs I p350

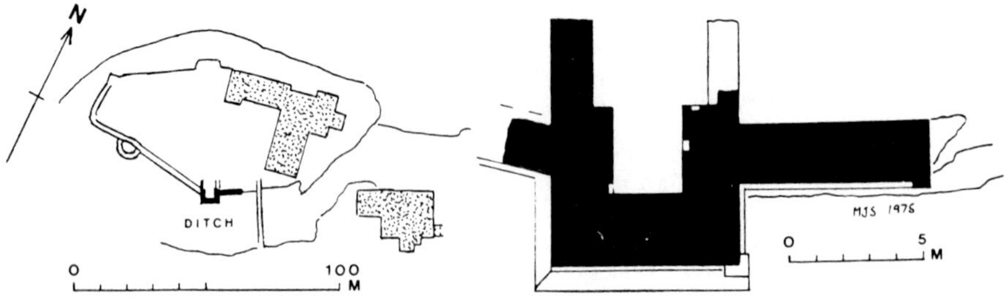

PLANS OF ALTON CASTLE

Alton Castle from the S.W.

ASHLEY CASTLE HILL

SJ 765375

The wooded hillock called Castle Hill to the north of the village of Ashley may be a natural feature utilised as a Norman motte.

AUDLEY MOTTE

SJ 799511

On the other side of the A52 north of the church is a natural hill which has been adapted to form a low 12th century castle mound with a maximum summit diameter of about 40m. This was the original seat of the de Audleys. Documentary references to this site in 1272-3 and 1275 suggest it was not immediately abandoned when the castle at Heighley was built in the 1220s, and excavations found a length of thin walling and a coin of the period 1272-1327.
See: Transactions of the North Staffs Field Club XLIX p92-6.

BIDDULPH MOTTE

SJ 889594

Excavation of the large conical earthwork at Lea Forge showed that it had been used as a castle mound in the 11th or 12th century. It was strengthened in the late 12th century and the dwelling upon it was rebuilt in the 13th century, and probably remained in use until Biddulph Hall was built in the late 16th century. The considerable remains of iron slag showed that there was a forge here in the later medieval period, hence the name Lea Forge.
See: Biddulph Historical Society No 1, June 1968, p6-9.

BURTON-ON-TRENT

The castle of 'Burt' mentioned in Domesday is probably an error for Burg, or Tutbury.

When Burton Abbey was dissolved in 1540 its buildings went to Lord Paget of Beaudesert, along with a licence to crenellate them, an unusual grant at such a late date. Among the Paget papers is a contemporary drawing of the Abbey with Tudor artillery bastions sketched in. The bastions may never have actually been built, but two "field pieces" are recorded at Burton in 1574 on the occasion of the forfeiture of Thomas, 3rd Lord Paget.

CAVERSWALL CASTLE

SJ 951428

A Thomas de Caverswall is recorded during Richard I's reign, but the deep and wide moat, now dry, and the lower parts of the outer walls probably date back to the time of Sir William de Caverswall, who was Sheriff of Staffordshire in 1260 and 1269, was licensed to crenellate Caverswall in 1275, and lived until 1292. In their present state the walls barely rise above the courtyard, which is roughly a square of 45m across. There are octagonal towers set on the corners, with another pair set either side of the gatehouse in the middle of the east side. The moat is very much wider on the west side. This would have helped to protect the apartments which are assumed to have originally lain on this side of the courtyard.

The Caverswall family seem to have preferred to live at High Ercall Hall in Shropshire in the 14th century, but in any case by the late 14th century Caverswall had passed to the Montgomeries. In c1515 the heiress Dorothy Montgomery married Sir Thomas Giffard, who later inherited Chillington Hall. Leland calls the castle at Caverswall a "pretty pile", but in Elizabeth I's reign it was let to a farmer called Browne, and allowed to decay.

In the early 17th century the castle was bought by the wealthy wool merchant Matthew Craddock, for whom in c1615 a fine new house was built in the northern part of the court, probably to designs by John Smythson, architect of Bolsover castle in Derbyshire. The upper parts of the towers were rebuilt with plain mullioned windows and they and the three storey house were finished off at the top with balustrading. That upon the house was replaced by battlements in the 19th century. The Craddocks held the castle for Parliament in the Civil War and it was captured by the Royalists in 1645.
See: Country Life Vol XXIX 1911 p886-95; T.N.S.F.C. 1937-8 p49-61.

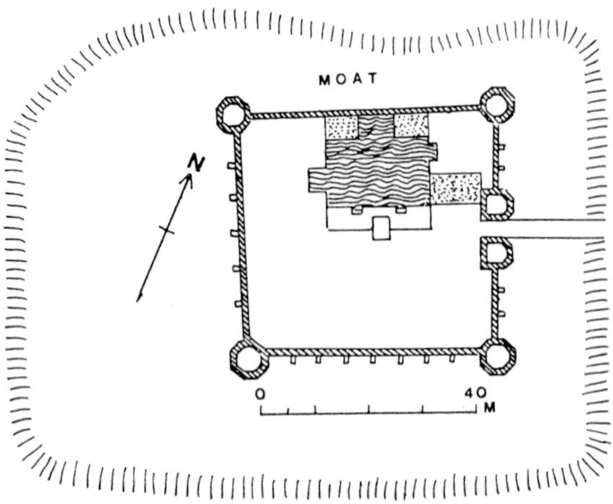

PLAN OF CAVERSWALL CASTLE

CHARTLEY CASTLE

SK 010285

Chartley belonged to the Earls of Chester from the end of the 11th century until 1232, when on Earl Ranulph de Blundeville's death it passed via his third daughter Agnes to William de Ferrers, Earl of Derby. The Ferrers family had had an interest in the castle in the 12th century, but in 1191-2 it was repaired and garrisoned by the Crown. The earthworks probably go back to the 1090s, but the stone keep and bailey curtain walls and towers were built in the 1220s by Earl Ranulph. They were presumably under construction in 1223 when the Earl was ordered by Henry III (with whom his relationship was then poor) to surrender his many castles. On the defeat of Robert de Ferrers at Chesterfield in 1266, Henry III gave Chartley to his younger son Edmund, but Robert seized the castle at night and held it until dispossessed by the King's forces. Edward I returned the castle to Robert in 1274. When William, 6th Baron Ferrers, died in 1450 Chartley passed to his daughter Anne and her husband Sir Walter Devereux, who in 1461 was summoned to Parliament as Baron Ferrers of Chartley, and was killed fighting alongside Richard III at the battle of Bosworth in 1485. However, by this period the castle was probably abandoned in favour of the moated mansion immediately to the west (see below) and in 1415 Leland describes it as a ruin.

The earthworks comprise a small motte at the west end, an inner bailey about 70m long by 50m wide, and an outer bailey roughly 56m square, separated by ditches, and with a ditch and an outer bank around the whole, which is set on a low ridge above the Uttoxeter to Stafford road. The motte is surmounted by the base of a large round tower keep now only about 2m high, but originally probably at least 16m high with three storeys. It measures 10.7m in internal diameter with walls 3.7m thick, and has facing the bailey slight remains of a projecting round stair turret about 7.8m in diameter. It would appear that the entrance was into this turret at first floor level from which the staircase started, the turret being solid below. Access down to the unlit storage basement of the keep is now by an internal stair, probably a later replacement of an earlier arrangement giving access down only through a trapdoor.

Chartley Castle

Chartley Castle:
The S.W. Tower
from the Keep.

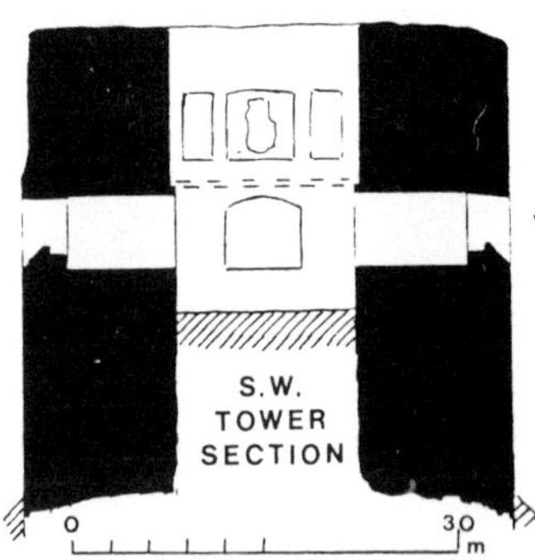

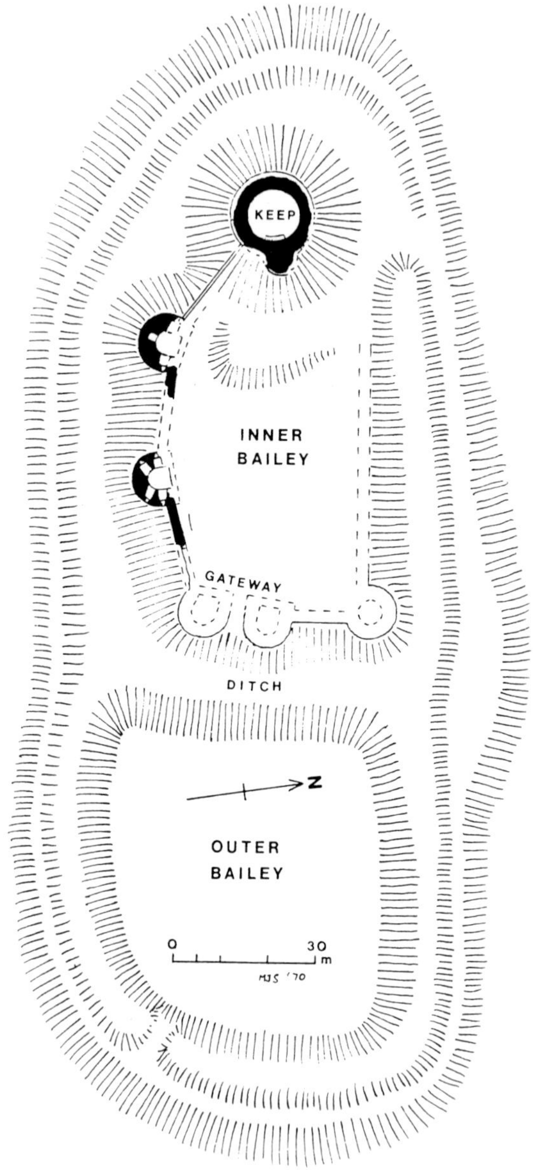

PLAN OF CHARTLEY CASTLE

The outer bailey shows no sign of stone defences but the inner bailey was defended by a stone curtain wall with five large and very massively constructed flanking towers. Only the defaced bases remain of the NE corner tower and the two towers flanking the gate which faced the outer bailey, although a higher fragment of the southern gateway tower, with evidence of two embrasures, remained in 1970. The curtain wall only remains standing in a fragmentary condition on the south side. The full thickness is difficult to ascertain at present, but was not less than 2m. However, there are impressive remains of the outer parts of the SW and south towers, with external diameters respectively of 12.5m and 11.7m and walls up to 4.2m thick. Each has slight traces of the former straight thin inner walls facing the courtyard, and contained three storeys, with two upper levels furnished with cross-shaped crossbow loops set over a low (now almost buried) basement without openings to the field. Altogether this castle was very strongly built.

It was probably in the mid 15th century that the castle became superseded by an embattled timber mansion set within a moat about 90m square on the lower ground immediately to the west. Towards the castle the moat broadens out into a large pool with two islands. A little way to the north is a second moated site with a dry ditch around a platform measuring 48m from SE to NW by 29m wide.

The great grandson of Sir Walter Devereux (see page 17) became the first Earl of Essex, and was a courtier of Elizabeth I, who was entertained at Chartley Hall in 1575. Against the wishes of his son, the second Earl of Essex, Mary, Queen of Scots was confined at the hall from December 1585 until September 1586, when she was transferred to Fotheringhay Castle for trial and execution. While at Chartley Mary had been plotting against Elizabeth, her messages to Anthony Babington being smuggled out of the hall in the false bottoms of beer casks. The second Earl of Essex later became Queen Elizabeth's favourite but he was executed and attainted after his abortive rebellion in 1601. His son Robert was only restored when James I succeeded in 1603. Robert took the side of Parliament in in the Civil War, but neither the hall nor the castle appear to have been involved in conflict. He died childless in 1646 and Chartley passed to his sister's grandson Sir Robert Shirley, created Baron Ferrers of Chartley in 1677, and made Earl Ferrers in 1711. The hall was accidentally burnt down in 1781 and the present house set on the west side of the moated platform is of 1847. The Shirley family remained owners of Chartley until the early 20th century.

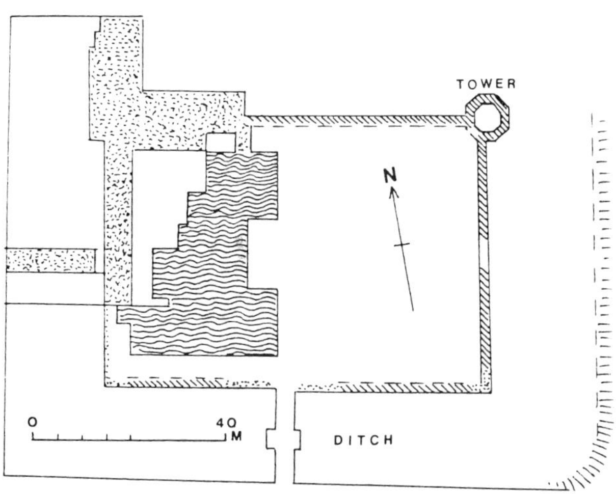

PLAN OF
ECCLESHALL

The east side of Eccleshall Castle.

ECCLESHALL CASTLE

SJ 828296

Eccleshall belonged to the Bishops of Coventry and Lichfield from an early period. In 1200 Bishop Muschamp was licensed by King John to fortify his manor house set on flat ground beside a stream to the north of the church. The enclosure of that period is thought to have been semi-circular in shape, and the present rectangular court was laid out by Walter Langton, Bishop from 1297 to 1321. He was Treasurer of England under Edward I, but was thrown into prison by Edward II, although later restored to office. Of his work there remains a three storey polygonal tower at the NE corner, the lower part of the 2m thick curtain wall on the north, east, and southern sides, the now dry east and southern arms of the moat, and perhaps the stone bridge with four breakwater buttresses on the south side. Originally there were probably towers on the other corners and on either side of the gateway in the south wall, and a hall and other chambers set on the north side of a court measuring about 75m long east to west by about 54m wide.

In 1642 Bishop Wright garrisoned the castle for Charles I. He died within it in 1643 while under siege from a Parliamentary force which occupied the parish church as a strongpoint. A royalist force arrived to relieve the castle and was on the point of taking away the Bishop's body, and the treasure in the castle, when a troop of Parliamentary horse arrived from Stafford, and the Royalists fled in confusion leaving only 10 men in the castle. They were forced to yield soon after when the gateway was captured in an assault at night, and in 1646 Parliament ordered the defences dismantled. The castle was later restored for further episcopal use, and in c1695 Bishop Lloyd built the present house on the west side of the court with a thirteen bay east facade with two shallow wings. There are later outbuildings to the west.

See: Renn p182; Pevsner p126; V.C.H. Staffs I p370.

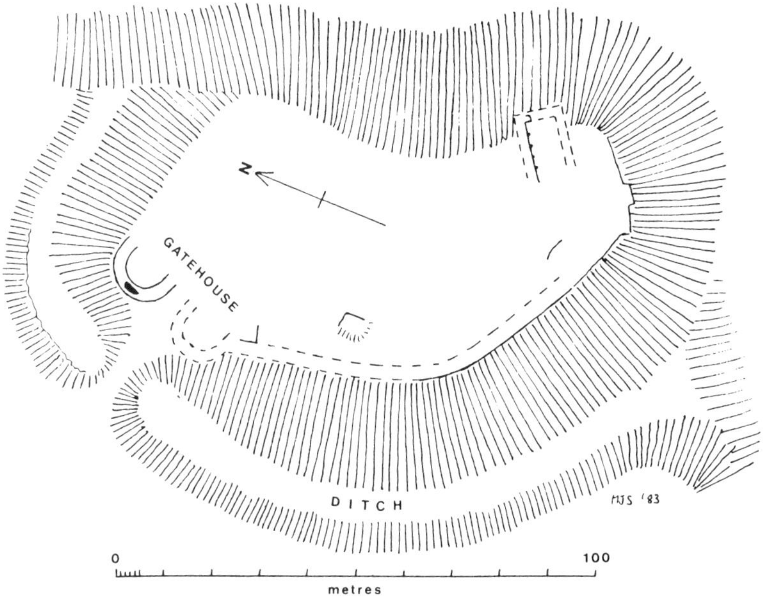

PLAN OF HEIGHLEY CASTLE

HAUGHTON MOTTE

SJ 865204

There are slight remains of an earthwork to the west of the parish church which may have been a small Norman motte. *See V.C.H. IV p136*

HEIGHLEY CASTLE

SJ 773467

Heighley Castle is spectacularly placed on a high wooded hill to the north of Madeley. It has an irregularly shaped courtyard over 100m long with a maximum width of 50m, with very steep falls to the east and south, and a deep ditch separating it from the rest of the hill on the other sides. Stone from the cutting of the ditch was used to build on the inner side a thick curtain wall of which footings only now remain under the soil. Overlooking a causeway across the ditch at the NW corner is a standing fragment and some foundations which suggest that there were once a pair of large D-shaped towers set either side of the gateway passage. The bailey area slopes markedly down towards the south end where there appear to have been a suite of domestic apartments. The exposed arcaded wall running from east to west formed the south wall of a vaulted undercroft which probably had a chamber of some importance, perhaps the solar, set above it.

The castle is generally understood to have been built by Henry de Audley, probably in the 1220s, and in imitation of the Earl of Chester's castle at Beeston. In 1223 de Audley was given a dozen hinds from the royal forest of Cannock to stock the park here, but the first certain mention of the castle is not until 1276. Early 14th century estimates of the value of the castle suggest it was then neglected, but it appears to have been still sufficiently in repair to be used as a prison in 1534, and to warrant demolition by Parliament in the Civil War to prevent its use by Royalists.
See: V.C.H. I p351

LICHFIELD CASTLE & CATHEDRAL CLOSE

SK 116097

A castle was built at Lichfield in 1129, and probably stood in the area of Ware Street and Frog Street. It was destroyed under the terms of a treaty of 1148. When Leland visited the town in c1540 the name Castle Field was still in use, and he comments on there having been a "castle of anciente tyme in the south part of the town, but no part of it standeth". The town seems to have once had a boundary ditch but Leland is adamant that "there is no token that ever the town was waullyd".

The rectangular cathedral close has a pair of wide pools on the south side, and on the other three sides had a ditch 30m wide by 5m deep, which still survives in an overgrown state on the north and east. This ditch was cut or recut by Bishop Roger de Clinton in c1130. Under the terms of a licence granted by Edward I to Bishop Walter Langton in 1299 the close was surrounded by an embattled wall with gateways on the west and south. Part of the west gateway survives, though without any features, plus parts of the north and east walls, a polygonal turret at the SE corner, and the lower part of a polygonal tower at the NE corner with a vaulted basement and much later patching in brick. Excavations still proceeding have shown that the southern gate, which faced a causeway between the two pools, had a pair of round flanking towers.

The SE corner turret of the Close.

The Close was garrisoned for the King in 1642. In March 1643 Lord Brooke was fatally wounded whilst leading an attack on the West Gate. Sir John Gell continued the attack with a bombardment from the south and the garrison yielded two days later. A month later Prince Rupert recaptured the Close after a ten day siege, and King Charles visited it three times in 1645. In 1646 Sir William Brereton besieged the Close from April until mid July, when under the surrender terms the garrison of 700 men with 85 officers, and other refugees, were permitted to leave. During the siege the cathedral central spire was brought down by cannon fire. By 1649 the Close, Cathedral, the Bishop's Palace in the NE corner, and many of the other buildings were wrecked. A new Bishop's Palace, on the same site but differently aligned, was built in 1687-8 and is now a school, and now much of the cathedral external stonework is 18th century and later.

See: V.C.H. Staffs XIV & I
S.Staffs Arch & Hist Soc XXV

The last remaining fragment of Madeley Manor House.

MADELEY MANOR HOUSE

SJ 773423

Ralph, Lord Stafford, was licensed to crenellate his manor house at Madeley in 1348, and the remains presumably date from that period. They lie on flat, boggy ground by a stream some way south of the village of Madeley. A wet moat enclosed a rectangular platform measuring about 80m from north to south by about 67m from east to west. The east and south arms of the moat are now only represented by shallow depressions, but the other two arms still contain over 12m width of water. Beyond them is a narrower outer wet moat on the west and a ditch containing the stream on the north, so originally there may have been a complete double circuit of wet moats. There are further outworks to the west. A walled courtyard and house occupied the NE corner of the plat- -form. all that remains of it is a length of the west wall of the court. It is 1.7m thick and has the southern jamb of a gateway which was closed by a portcullis.

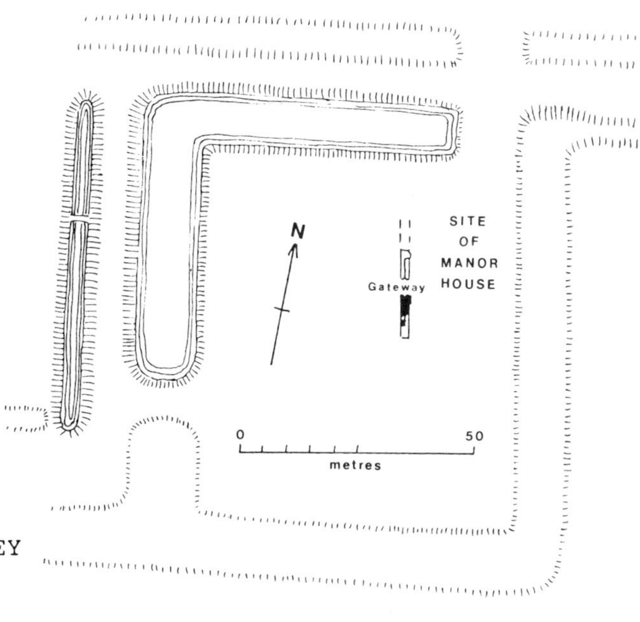

PLAN OF MADELEY MANOR HOUSE

NEWCASTLE-UNDER-LYME CASTLE SJ 844459

The date and circumstances of the founding of this castle are not known. It may have been built by Henry I in the early 12th century and named Newcastle as being a substitute for the former royal castle at Stafford, with the appendage 'under Lyme' from the tract of forest of that name in the adjacent part of Cheshire. Newcastle was one of several castles held by Ralph Gernons, Earl of Chester, which were surrendered to King Stephen after the Earl was captured at Northampton in 1146, and an alternative origin for it is that he was the builder. Newcastle was restored to the Earl in 1149 and he was confirmed in his extensive estates at Henry II's accession in 1154, although the King took the castle back and retained it after the Earl's murder by William Peveril later in the same year.

There are many records of expenditure by Henry II, Richard I, and John on maintenance and garrisons at Newcastle, and there was a rectangular tower keep, and probably some other stone buildings, by 1192. King John spent over £200 on the castle, visited it in 1206, and in 1215 granted it to the Earl of Chester. On the Earl's death in 1232 Henry III recovered the castle. In 1264 Henry granted it to his captor Simon de Montfort, Earl of Leicester, who in 1265 was defeated and killed at the battle of Evesham. Henry's younger son Edmund, Earl of Lancaster, was given Newcastle in 1267, and the connection between Newcastle and the Duchy of Lancaster thus began lasted until the present century.

John of Gaunt, Duke of Lancaster, had repairs made to Newcastle in the 1370s and the Duchy accounts suggest it was well maintained until the 1440s, after which Henry VI neglected it in favour of Tutbury, although minor repairs were carried out in 1478-9. Leland in c1541 says that "All the castel is doune save one great toure". The buildings were "altogether decayed" by 1610 when leased to the Sneyd family. In 1828 they purchased the site from the Duchy and drained and reclaimed the marshy land which had formerly been the castle pool.

Over a century and a half ago there was still extant a book of Chaucer's poems published in 1602 into which a few years later had been written a description of the castle. "......New Castle was no more nor 150 paces fro south to north, but well nigh two hundred from est to west; and had two transepts and four bays with dungen tower of twentie paces square, which rose in three storeys of full height of seventy feet....a low portal, and not well lighted passage did admit to the hall, very large and spacious, with roof loftie, and painted with devices, galleries for the minstralls, and the walls clothed with geer of warfare...wending a gloomy staircase did lead to the state rooms and bedd-chamber of the Prince, and other on the upper for the companie...The walls outer had good buttresses to the height of thirty feet and the whole was moer fytt as a statelie comfortable dwellinge then as a fortress of defence, cause of the rising landes south and este...."

All that now remains of the castle is part of the much reduced mound squeezed in between a factory and a bowling green alongside Silverdale Road. The bailey site, now covered with housing, was to the north, while the other three sides were protected by a lake created by damming the Lyme Brook. This area is now covered with a thick layer of silt. Excavations have revealed the foundations of a long narrow building SW of the mound, and a long wall with a chamfered plinth and buttresses to the north of the mound.

See: T.Pape - Medieval Newcastle-Under-Lyme; Renn p254
V.C.H. Staffs I p353, VIII 11-15

RODBASTON HALL

SJ 921124

The hereditary forester of Cannock had a castle in this area in 1154. In 1199 it is mentioned as a manor house, and as a castle again in 1215. The existing remains appear to be relics of a moated and crenellated house built by John Saundersted, probably in c1330-40. They comprise a moat with about 6m width of water enclosing an overgrown tree-clad platform about 50m square with a mound about 4m high on the SE side which is probably covering the debris and ruins of stone buildings. There is a gap in the moat, wider than it was formerly, towards the west end of the south side. The manor of Rodbaston was subsequently held by a series of families but the house appears to have been occupied by the Eginton family as tenants from the 1380s until c1768. *See VCH V p120-2*

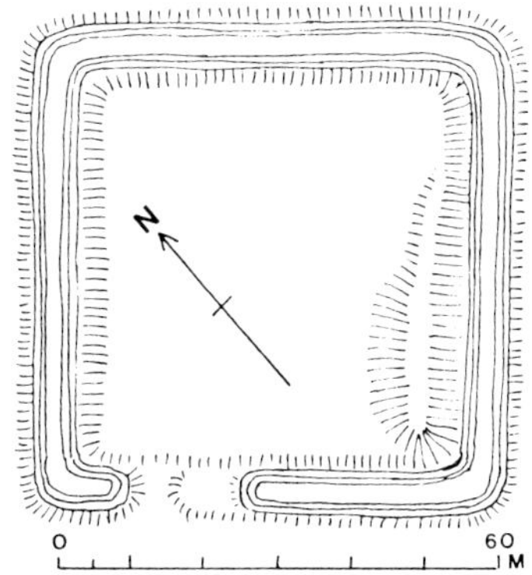

PLAN OF RODBASTON HALL

STAFFORD CASTLE

SJ 902222

There has been quite considerable confusion in the past about the relationship between the present castle site 2km west of Stafford, and the castle that is known to have existed in the town. It is now generally accepted that the castle built by King William in 1070 stood on the west side of the town within the area defended by the River Sow, and that traces or memories of its site survived until c1600. In 1071 many manors in Staffordshire, including the manor of Bradley, which adjoins Stafford, were granted to Roger de Toeni, whose son adopted the surname de Stafford. It was undoubtedly the latter who raised substantial earthworks on the present site. The castle recorded in Domesday Book (1086) as recently destroyed was presumably the old royal castle, and the castle entrusted by Henry I to William Pantulf in 1102 was probably the new baronial castle.

The baronial castle is mentioned in the 1140s. Evidence has now come to light that a stone rectangular tower keep was built on the mound sometime in the 12th century, probably by Robert de Stafford. He died in 1188, leaving an heiress Millisent, who married Hervey Bagot, who then adopted the Stafford surname to continue the line.

It was Ralph, Lord Stafford, who revived the family fortunes. In 1347 he made an agreement with the mason John de Burcestre for the construction on the mound of a substantial stone tower house with octagonal corner towers, and in 1348 Edward III licensed him to embattle and fortify it. The death of Edmund, Earl of Stafford at the battle of Shrewsbury in 1403 left an infant heir, Humphrey. He married into the Buckingham family in 1444, thus obtaining wide estates with many castles, and the title of Duke of Buckingham. In 1521 King Henry VIII executed and attainted Edward Stafford, third Duke of Buckingham, on trumped up charges of treason because he had a distant claim to the throne. Then, and again in 1537, inventories of the Stafford estates were drawn up which give a wealth of detail about the buildings and their furnishings at their many castles. Although they lost their two main titles, the Staffords recovered Stafford Castle, and became barons of Stafford again in 1547.

The Mound and Tower House ruins, Stafford Castle.

In 1575 Queen Elizabeth was entertained to dinner at Stafford Castle after she had visited the town. However, the family had not recovered their former wealth and the buildings became neglected, being described as the "rotten castle of Stafford" in 1603, and as "somewhat ruined" in 1634. In 1639 the impoverished heir surrendered the barony to Charles I, who then granted it to Sir William Howard, husband of Mary Stafford, although the elderly Isabel, Lady Stafford was still living in the tower house when the Civil War broke out. She fortified it for the King, and a minor skirmish in the vicinity in May 1643 was followed by a siege until July, when the garrison withdrew. At the end of the year the Parliamentary Committee at Stafford ordered the castle to be "forthwith demolished".

In the 18th century the NE corner tower of the tower house, which had remained standing higher than the rest after slighting, was converted into a folly. A new Earldom of Stafford, created for Henry Howard in 1688 became extinct in 1762, but a descendant of the last Earl through the female line, Sir George Jerningham, obtained a revival of the barony in 1824. In c1812-15 he had the tower house ruins cleared of debris, measured, and then, on the understanding it would help his claim to the title, commenced its restoration. By 1817 Edward Jerningham was inhabiting a suite of rooms at the east end, and the eastern towers had been restored to about their original height. On obtaining the title, however, the family ceased work on what promised to be a less comfortable seat than their other residences. The castle was left to deteriorate and the last caretakers left in 1950, when it was declared unsafe. In 1961 a boy playing at the castle was killed by the collapse of the mullions of the main east window. The Borough Council demolished the upper parts of the restored building but luckily resisted the demands from some quarters for complete demolition, and from 1978 began archeological exploration, and the laying out of the grounds as an ancient monument and public amenity.

Ralph, Lord Stafford, as depicted on the brass of Sir Hugh Hastings, d1347 at Elsing in Norfolk.

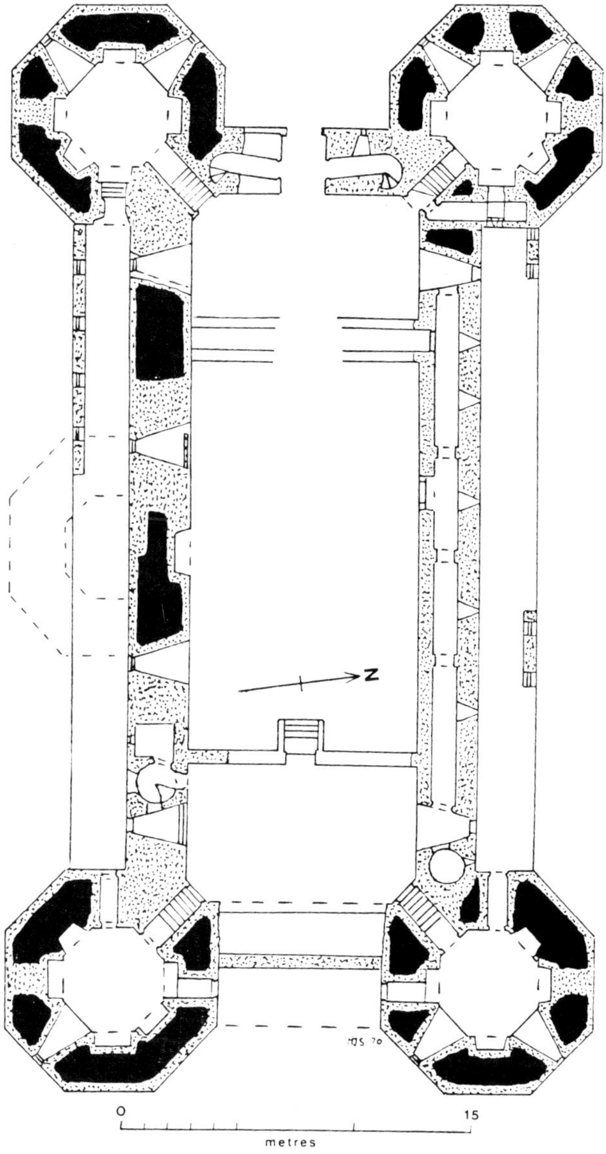

PLAN OF STAFFORD CASTLE

The earthworks at Stafford Castle are large and impressive. The mound has a summit about 65m long from east to west by 40m wide. It was originally isolated from the D-shaped bailey to the NE by a ditch. The bailey measures over 100 metres across from the east, where there is a sunken entrance, to the west. It is known that in the bailey throughout the medieval period there were apartments, a kitchen, stables, a chapel of St Nicholas, barns and other storage and service buildings probably built of an assortment of materials, but no evidence has been found of a stone curtain wall around them.

The excavations found evidence that in the Civil War the whole of the inner bailey was regarded as too large an area to defend with the available forces, and that part of it was refortified with earth and timber with the aid of gambions (wicker baskets filled with earth). To the east is an even larger outer bailey probably used only as a garden or for agricultural purposes in the late medieval period. Beyond it, extending nearly to St Mary's church, are traces of a settlement occupied from the 12th century to the 14th century.

What was then considered as a dangerous 19th century ruin on the mound only escaped total demolition in the 1960s because of a suspicion that it might still incorporate 14th century work. The excavations begun in 1978 have indeed shown this to be true. It is now known that the mound was originally given a much smaller round summit at a higher level and in the 1340s this was shaved down to the internal size of the tower house which was then built against it. This effectively gave a solid basement, except for a small wine cellar let into the mound. The surplus earth was then piled on the west side of the mound to support one end of a structure 34.4m long by 14.8m wide over walling which is rather thicker than the 7ft (2.1m) stipulated in the contract of 1347. However, this somewhat conflicts with the evidence that the western 10m of the tower was built over the remains of, or incorporated, a late 12th century tower keep, unless it is accepted that the latter was originally built against the mound slope, as at Clun Castle in Shropshire.

The new tower house had two main storeys, the lower level being for servants, and the storage and preparation of food and drink, and the upper level containing the great hall in the centre with the solar at its west end. The octagonal corner towers some 9m in diameter appear to have contained four storeys of private rooms, corresponding in level to the solid basement, the two main storeys, and the wallwalk level of the main block. All the rooms except the topmost are recorded as having fireplaces. The plan made before the rebuilding shows a service stair in the walling of the NW tower, but there was uncertainty as to the exact position of the entrance and how access was obtained up to the hall. These were presumably in the north wall, which was then almost gone, and in the rebuilding was provided with a mural gallery. The contract of 1347 specified that the battlements were to be carried out from the walls with machicolation slots behind the parapet, as at the slightly later Guy's Tower at Warwick Castle. When the 19th century restoration work was stopped only the east end was completed. The remainder only stood to its present height and was left open as a garden. The entrance at the west end replaced an original postern doorway.

The town of Stafford was naturally protected by the River Sow on the west and south, and by streams and marshland on the other two sides. In 913 Ethelfleda surrounded the town with earth banks reinforced with timber. In the 1220s and 30s Henry III encouraged the rebuilding of the walls, probably in stone, although two early 17th century maps show that part of the NW side, and nearly all of the western side of the town were still only protected by earthen banks and stockades at the time of the Civil War. This may be how picked Parliamentarian troopers were able to infiltrate and capture the town so easily in 1643. The maps show an opening on the west, rectangular gabled gatehouses without battlements on the south and east, and a more impressive gatehouse with twin round embattled towers on the north. The walls were ruinous by the 1670s. The North Gate was replaced by a house of correction late in the 17th century, the South Gate was demolished in 1777, and the East Gate was taken down in c1800 leaving a fragment of the north wall which was moved to its present position in 1939, and is the sole relic of the walls.

See: V.C.H. Staffs Vols I & VI; Renn p315, Salt Arch Soc VIII p6-22

STOURTON CASTLE

SO 859849

The royal forest of Kinver probably had a hunting lodge in this area by the reign of William II. A ditch was dug around the lodge in 1184-5, and the courtyard enclosed, presumably by a palisade, in 1185-6. Work was done on the King's chamber in 1187-8, and further work on the buildings in 1190-1. A fresh set of timber buildings on a new site at Stourton were erected in 1195-6. They included a hall and offices, a kitchen, a chamber, a gaol, and a gate with a brattice, and were surrounded with a palisade 16 feet high with a circumference of 16 perches. King John came here to hunt in 1207 and 1215. By 1222 the lodge was known as the castle of Kinver and John, son of Phillip, the King's Forester for Kinver, fortified it with funds and timber provided by Henry III.

Sir John Vaux was made Keeper of Kinver Forest and Stourton castle in 1310, and in 1316 was implicated in the murder there of Sir Thomas Murdak. Vaux was aquitted, although he had subsequently married Sir Thomas's widow Gillian, who was sentenced to be burnt. In 1360 the Prior of Dudley was held at Stourton for an offence against the strict forest laws.

In 1382 Richard de Hampton succeeded Hugh Tyrell as Lord of Kinver, and in 1391 his son John was licensed to have an oratory at Stourton Castle. His elder son, also called John, was a courtier of Henry VI. He held a number of important offices from the 1430s until 1461, and probably rebuilt the castle in that period. He was ejected from his offices and estates when the Duke of York seized the throne as Edward IV in 1461, but recovered Stourton for a short while in 1470 when Henry VI was briefly restored. He died two years later, and Edward IV gave Stourton to his brother George, Duke of Clarence, by whom it was briefly alienated to Tewkesbury Abbey but recovered by Henry VII.

In c1500 the castle is thought to have been the home of Sir Reginald Pole and his wife Margaret, daughter of the late Duke of Clarence. Their son Reginald is generally considered to have been born here around that time. He was favoured by his relative Henry VIII, who gave him various clerical offices. Later, however, he opposed Henry's divorce, and retired to Rome, where he was created a cardinal and sent to persuade Spain and France to invade England. Pole survived attempts by King Henry's agents to murder him and returned as Archbishop of Canterbury when England was returned to allegiance with Rome under Queen Mary. With impeccable timing he died a few hours after her in 1558.

Stourton Castle from the west.

Tamworth Castle: The Shell Keep from the South

During the first two thirds of the 17th century the castle was occupied by the Whorwood family, who also had a second residence at Compton, NW of Kinver, until it was sold in 1650. John Whorwood appears to have remained neutral in the Civil War, but in 1644 the castle was taken by a Parliamentary force under Colonel Thomas Fox. It was surrendered back to the Royalists after Colonel Fox was routed on Stourbridge Heath by Sir Gilbert Gerard, the Governor of Worcester. The defences were probably destroyed soon afterwards, and 18th century views show a many-gabled house standing on a flat platform with a buttresses retaining wall on the north and eastern sides, presumably the lower part of the original curtain wall.

The nearby mill was converted into a forge in c1650 and the noise and vibration from it made Stourton Castle unsuitable as a residence for gentry. Throughout much of the 18th century it was occupied by a farming family called Hollins, whilst in the 19th it was occupied by a succession of industrialists. The castle was sold in 1974 and remains occupied as a private residence.

Stourton Castle stands on an outcrop with the River Stour to the east and slopes to the north and south. The house stands on the site of a keep or small inner court, the space being now all roofed over. On the west side is a square tower which dates from the 14th or 15th century and is similar to the surviving tower at Holt Castle in Worcestershire, although externally disguised with rendering. The remaining ranges around the former court are of brick and were built in the mid to late 16th century, although the gables are of the 17th century. The hall lay on the east side and had a porch tower which was demolished in the 1830s when Sir Robert Smirke was employed to oversee very considerable alterations and additions, including the mock Jacobean wings projecting to the west. A walled court had been created in this side in the late 17th century. In 1832 the foundations of a pair of round towers of an outer bailey to the NW were discovered. These may have been part of the work authorised by Henry III in the 1220s.

See: V.C.H. Staffs I p369, XX p130-2

SWYNNERTON CASTLE

SJ 853354

Edward II licensed Roger de Swynnerton to crenellate his house here in 1315, but it is not known if any defences were actually built or which site would have been thus enclosed. The present hall dates from the 1720s and was built for Thomas Fitzherbert.

TAMWORTH CASTLE

SK 207039

King Offa, who ruled Mercia from 757 to 796, is said to have made Tamworth his capital, building a palace there, and surrounding the town with a rampart and ditch. It remained the capital of Mercia until 874, when it was destroyed by the Danes and lay derelict for several decades. In 912 King Edward the Elder permitted his sister Ethelfleda to govern Mercia which by then had become a province within his kingdom. Excavations carried out at various occasions in this century have established that the boundary of the medieval town originated with the earth and timber defences she had erected in 913. Her nephew Athelstan, King of England from 924 to 940, made Tamworth one of his seats, but the town was destroyed again in 943 by the Danes, and was never again a royal residence, although there was a royal mint in the town until the 12th century.

On the strength of this association with the Saxon Kings the castle mound at Tamworth has been erronously described as of Saxon origin. However, it is obviously a typical Norman artificial castle mound, and was probably raised in the late 11th century by Robert Marmion. He is said to have held Tamworth, and also the manor of Scrivelsby in Lincolnshire, on condition of performing the office of royal champion, a hereditary post requiring the holder to come to coronations dressed for combat and "oppose himself against any person who should gainsay the royal coronation".

King John ordered the destruction of Tamworth Castle because Robert Marmion, 5th baron, sided with the barons against him at the time of Magna Carta, but this was evidently not carried out. The Marmion male line failed in 1294, and Edward I later granted the castle to Sir Alexander de Freville. He was royal champion at the coronation of Edward III in 1327. The King was then a minor, and this is the only certain occasion when the role of royal champion was actually performed, and the office was subsequently attached to the manor of Scrivelsby, which had passed to a younger daughter of the last male Marmion.

In 1423 Tamworth Castle passed by marriage from the Frevilles to Sir Thomas Ferrers, son of the 5th Baron Ferrers of Groby in Leicestershire. His successors continued to use the keep as an occasional residence, and were carrying out repairs to it in 1541 when Leland visited the town. He records that the "base-court and great ward of the Castle is cleane decayed and the wall fallen downe, and therein be now but houses of office of noe notable building".

The castle was visited three times by James I towards the end of his reign. On the second occasion he was accompanied by Prince Charles, who stayed at the Moat House to the west. The castle was garrisoned for King Charles in 1642 and was taken by Parliamentary forces in 1643. Somehow the keep managed to avoid being slighted.

In 1688 Ann Ferrers, heiress of Tamworth Castle, married Robert Shirley, heir of Baron Ferrers of Chartley, thus reuniting the two branches of the family. Their daughter and heiress married James Crompton, fifth Earl of Northampton, in 1715, and in 1751 another heiress brought the castle to George Townsend, who in 1786 became Marquis Townsend. These families had residences elsewhere and used the castle but rarely. In the 1790s the hall in the keep was leased to the industrialist Robert Peel for use as a forge in connection with the factory he had built nearby. In the Jubilee year of 1897 Tamworth Corporation purchased the castle from the Marquis Towns--end. The former bailey was then laid out as a public garden with a bandstand, and the keep was renovated, and in 1899 opened as the town museum.

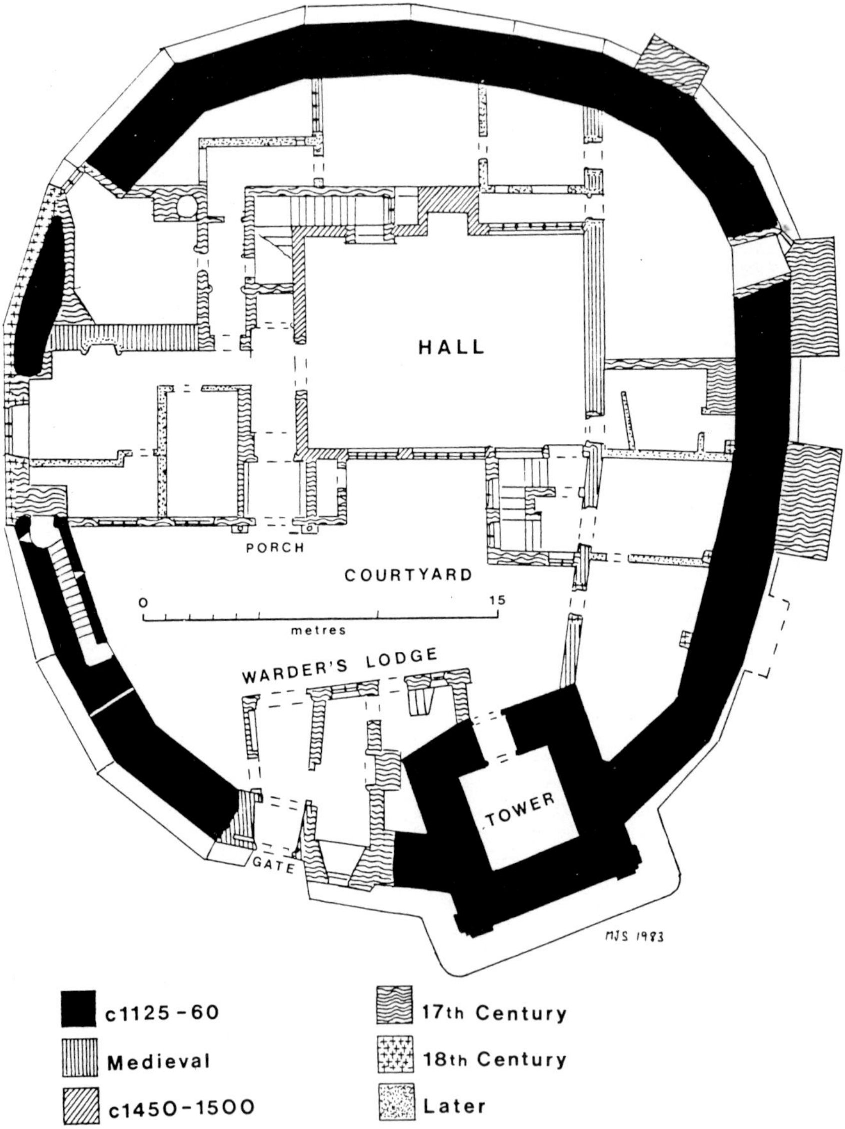

PLAN OF TAMWORTH CASTLE

Tamworth Castle: Curtain wall with herringbone masonry

Tamworth Castle: The entrance porch to the domestic buildings.

The castle lies between the north bank of the River Tame and the main street of the town. As laid out in the late 11th century it comprised a large artificial mound standing at the NW corner of a quadrangular bailey about 90m long from east to west, with the east and west sides about 35m and 60m long respectively. Excavations have revealed post holes of the original timber defences of the bailey. Nothing survives of the buildings within the bailey, although some excavation near the bandstand has revealed the foundations of 16th century stables and outbuildings. In 1972-4 the interesting lowest storey of a gatehouse of c1260 on the north side close to the NE corner was revealed and left exposed. It has a sort of flattened heart shape with rounded portions flanking the entrance, and is of fine ashlar. The surviving part was at moat level, the actual gate being at the next level, with at least one more storey above. It was originally approached by a timber bridge with a drawbridge at the inner end, but in the early 14th century the part of the bridge next the drawbridge was rebuilt in stone, and was again rebuilt in the early 16th century. The upper portions of the gatehouse were demolished in c1700 and the lower part incorporated in the cellars of the Town Hall Vaults public house, which was removed in c1970.

Crossing the motte ditch is a short but interesting section of curtain walling 2.7m thick, the walkway on top of which formed the only access to the keep on the motte. This wall has extensive courses of herringbone masonry, a feature found in a number of Late Saxon and Early Norman churches, but very rarely in castles. Here it is unlikely to be earlier than c1100 or later than c1150.

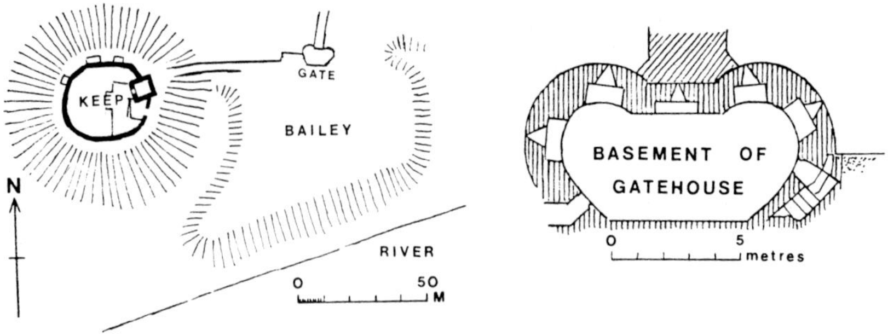

PLANS OF TAMWORTH CASTLE

The polygonal shell wall of coursed rubble with a high battered plinth without quoins is likely to be of the same period, or only slightly later than the approach wall, say c1125-60. Although some breaches have been made in it for later openings, the shell wall is one of the best preserved and least altered of its type in Britain. Above the plinth it is about 2.3m thick, and rises 7.4m to a wall--walk which is protected by a parapet 3.8m high. Within it is an area 31m from east to west by 28m north to south. this is slightly larger than many other shell keeps and has proved large enough to accommodate a dwelling thought adequate throughout later centuries, which may account for the preservation of this shell wall when many others were ruinous before the end of the medieval period.

Projecting slightly from the shell, commanding the approach, is a contemporary tower with walls about 2m thick around an unlit basement roughly 4m square, although the walls are much thinner at higher levels. The outer corners of the tower have typical Norman pilaster buttresses set slightly back, and, thanks to much later remodelling, these are finished off at the top by round turrets. The existing gateway arch near the tower is later medieval in its present form, and is surmounted by a Jacobean building called the Warder's Lodge. A window embrasure on the north side of the shell is thought to have been adapted from a former postern doorway.

Originally there would have been lean-to buildings around the inner face of the shell, with the hall perhaps where the kitchen and service rooms are on the north. Walling in these ranges may be earlier than the later 15th century hall with its long axis set north to south, and parallel to, but clear of, the west side. This leaves a narrow court between it and the gateway. The hall has been much remodelled, and the entrance porch, the staircases at the SW and NE corners, and much of the domestic apartments south of it, were erected by Sir John Ferrers during James I's reign. Further alterations were carried out after the Civil War, and in the 18th century, including the projections from the shell with big windows.
See: H.Wood - A guide to Tamworth Castle; Renn p319; Pevsner p277

TRENTHAM CASTLE

A "castellum de Trentham' is mentioned in the Pipe Rolls for 1168. This may refer to a castle here also commemorated by the placename Mount Field, but it could also be an alternative name for the royal stronghold at Newcastle-Under-Lyme.

TUTBURY CASTLE

SK 209291

The castle at Tutbury occupies a splendid defensive site above the River Dove that may have been utilised in Saxon times. However, the existing earthwork defences were created shortly after the Norman Conquest of 1066. William I gave Tutbury to Hugh de Avranches, but in 1071 transferred it to Henry, Lord of Ferriers and Chambrais in Normandy, first of the line of nobles known in England as the de Ferrers. The castle appears to have been his principal residence, and was the administration centre for the over two hundred manors that he held. By the castle stood a town mentioned in Domesday Book, and part of its ancient boundary rampart and ditch still remains.

Robert de Ferrers, the third son of Henry, was created Earl of Derby in 1138. The third Earl, William, joined the rebellion of Henry II's sons against their father, and the castle was besieged and taken by Henry II in 1174, and destroyed a year later. Tutbury Castle was subsequently rebuilt in stone, and the shell keep that once surmounted the motte, and the chapel in the bailey, were built probably between then and the end of the 12th century.

Earl Robert de Ferrers supported Simon de Montfort against Henry III, and in 1263 Prince Edward laid waste his lands and did much damage to Tutbury Castle. After the rebel barons' defeat at Evesham in 1265 the Earl lost his possessions, and Tutbury went to Edmund, Henry III's younger son, created Earl of Lancaster in 1267. Edmund or his son Thomas built a new suite of apartments at the south end of the bailey. These included a hall over 18m long and a great chamber 14m long, both being nearly 9m wide, and they stood until the end of the 16th century. In 1313-4 Earl Thomas spent £100 on building the existing gateway tower. He led the baronial opposition to Edward II, and was defeated at Burton in 1322, and captured and executed the same year. Tutbury Castle was plundered but most of the Earl's money was lost in the River Dove while being carted away, and was not found until the 19th century.

In 1326 Edward II returned Tutbury to Thomas's brother Henry, whose heiress Blanche married Edward III's third son John of Gaunt, then created Duke of Lancaster. John of Gaunt was often abroad, in London, or at one of his many other castles, but Tutbury seems to have been well used by his wife, and repairs are recorded in 1362, and some new walling in the 1390s. When John of Gaunt died in 1399 Richard II seized the Duchy of Lancaster, which has belonged to the sovereign ever since. However, the same year saw the return of John of Gaunt's exiled heir, who deposed Richard and took the crown as Henry IV. A new tower, which has not survived, was being built at the time of Henry's visits in 1404 and 1405, and work on a fresh section of curtain walling was begun prior to his death in 1413. Under Henry VI much of the present curtain wall around the bailey was built, the work being started at the southern end in 1420. It proceeded slowly until 1442, when the South Tower was begun. From 1446 to 1461 Tutbury was held by his Queen, Margaret of Anjou, the South Tower being finished in the 1450s, and the North tower being under construction in 1457-60.

However, the castle was fast approaching obsolescence as both a fortress and residence as subsequent kings had little use for it. The shell keep was totally ruinous by the end of the century, the kitchen roof fell down by 1516, and by 1523 many roofs were leaking and a 30m long section of the curtain wall between the North Tower and the gatehouse was split lengthways from top to bottom. In 1559 a surveyor called the castle "indifferently" well repaired, but a sketch of the castle made in c1560 shows it looking magnificent enough, and finally, in 1561, repairs were at last put in hand.

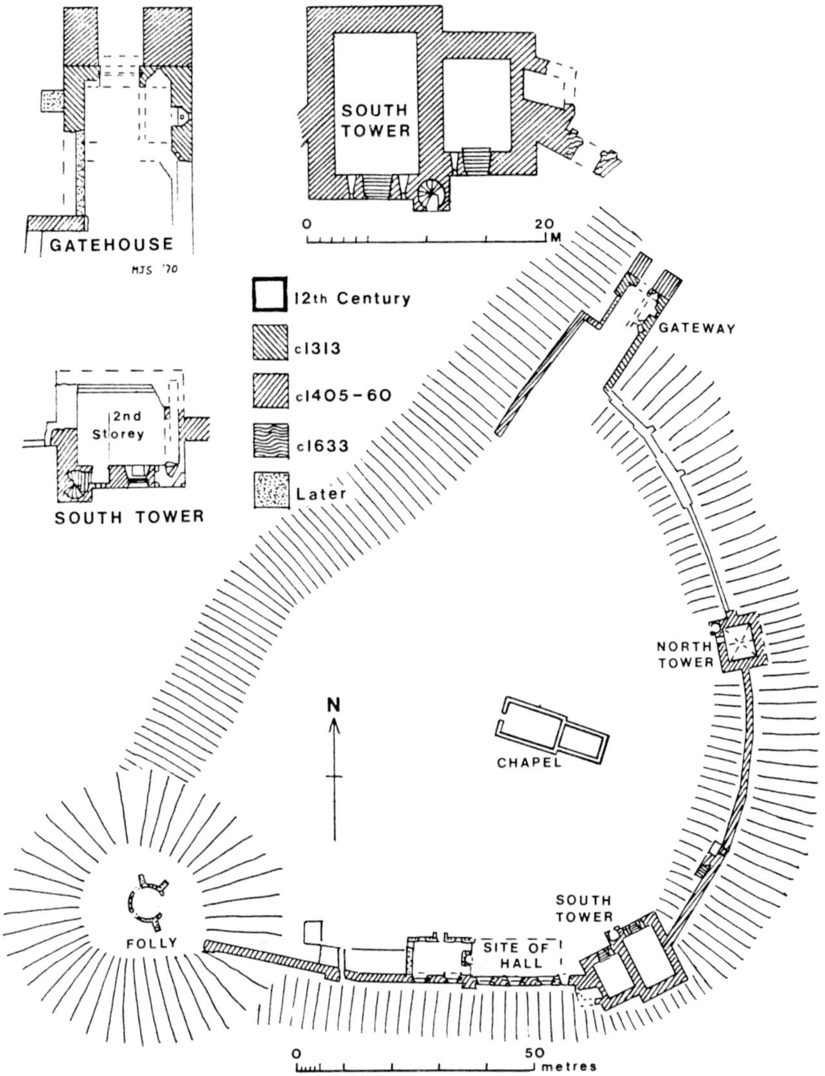

PLANS OF TUTBURY CASTLE

Considerable repairs and preparations were necessary at Tutbury to make the castle suitable for incarcerating Mary, Queen of Scots, who was under the charge of the Talbot Earl of Shrewsbury. She was accommodated in the medieval apartments from February to June 1569, the hall and chamber being subdivided with wainscotted partitions to make them more amenable to her. After short stays at Wingfield and Coventry she returned to Tutbury for the first half of 1570.

Tutbury Castle: The Gatehouse.

In 1585 Mary was again at Tutbury under the charge of Sir Ralph Sadler, Chancellor of the duchy of Lancaster. He stayed in the old apartments where Mary had previously been, and she was accommodated on the upper floor of a freestanding range which once stood to the south of the North Tower. She complained of the stench of a nearby privy without a drain that was emptied only once a week and of her only privacy being in two small rooms with windows only facing the "dark surrounding walls". Sir Ralph did what he could to make life tolerable for Mary, taking her riding and hawking, but in April he was replaced by Sir Amyas Paulet, a Puritan who was stricter with the captive Queen, and who took up residence in the suite of rooms over the gateway so as to overlook the town and the approaches.

In the 1590s the outer gateway of the lower court was reported almost roofless, and the North Tower was badly cracked. Probably some repairs were made as King James visited Tutbury several times to enjoy hawking in Needwood Forest, and in the 1630s the medieval main apartments were replaced by a new two storey range for which large windows were pierced through the old outer wall. Charles I was at Tutbury in 1634 and other years. It was garrisoned for him in 1642, and withstood a short siege the following year. Charles and Prince Rupert were at the castle in 1645 but the following year it was surrendered to Parliament in April after a three week siege. Demolition of the walls was begun in 1647.

Some of the accommodation at the castle was patched up in 1662 and leased to the Duke of Ormonde. From 1681 until 1864 the castle was leased to the Vernon family. A new house, incorporating some older materials, was built beside the site of the medieval hall in the 1750s, and follies, or eye catchers, were built on top of the motte and the South Tower. Recent excavations have shown that the inner part of the eastern rampart is a landscaped feature of this era raised over the debris of the slighted curtain wall and the remains of buildings that once stood against it on the inner side. The house was altered and extended in the 19th century and is still used by the resident caretaker. The Duchy carried out repairs to the ruins in 1832, and the system of admitting paying visitors was introduced as early as 1847 because of wear and tear from tourists.

Tutbury castle has a D-shaped inner bailey with a mound at the south end, a steep drop to the river on the straight NW side, and a deep and wide ditch around the other sides, with also a rampart on the east. The original approach was up the deep gully dividing the two large outer enclosures on the east and NE sides. The latter is now the visitors' car park and the other is now a field, but was a garden in the time of Mary, Queen of scots. The present approach from the town is by the south, skirting the outer edge of the main ditch. It leads up to the gatehouse, a rectangular tower 11m by 8m externally with solid rectangular turrets added in front of it in the 15th century. The entrance arch is asymetrically placed so as to allow the passageway to be flanked by a narrow room for a guard or porter on the south side. Only one upper storey remains, but there is evidence that there were originally at least two.

The curtain wall from the gateway to the North Tower, and then on by a small turret and stair to the South Tower, only survives to chest height. The first section south of the gateway shows signs of needing repeated rebuilding and repair, probably because of poor foundations. The North Tower measures 10.6m by 9.6m externally. It has a vaulted basement now almost buried in the rampart and having its own entrance direct from the court. A second entrance gave onto the foot of a spiral stair in a square turret to the self contained suite of three pleasant upper rooms with large windows facing the court, and latrines in the SE corner. These chambers are now very ruined but the turret stands nearly to the full original height.

The South Tower is a double tower with the western part similar in design and size to the North Tower, but the eastern part is much larger. Although probably intended to dominate the town the tower was evidently finished off at its present height with only two storeys. Above two cellars which were intended to be vaulted are two fine chambers with fireplaces in the side walls, the lintels for which were ordered in 1449. Close to the west is the site of the medieval hall, and in the middle of the court are foundations of a freestanding Norman chapel. The chancel may have been extended later. In front of the present house is a well over 36m deep.
See: The Guide to Tutbury Castle by Sir Robert Somerville, *1964*.

WESTON JONES MOTTE SJ 768243

By a stream NE of the hamlet of Weston Jones in Norbury parish is a low and worn down motte. See also Page 12.

WOLSELEY HALL SK 034204

In 1469 Edward IV licensed Ralph Wolseley to crenellate his house here in the Trent Valley between Colwich and Rugeley, but it is not known if anything was thus constructed. The present hall does not appear to be of great age, although the Wolseley family have lived here since at least the 11th century to the present century. The pool to the west may be associated with a former moat.

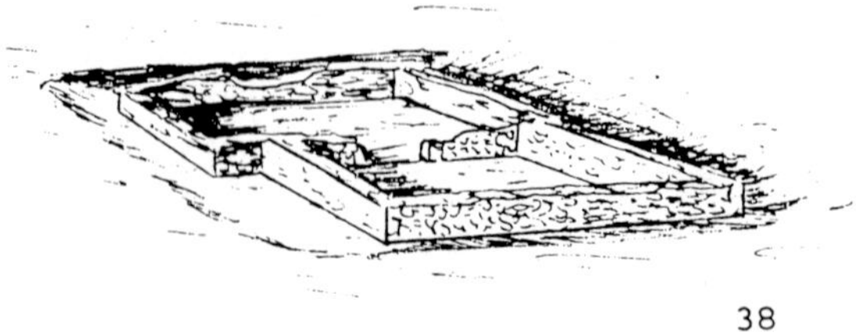

Tutbury Castle: The Chapel

MOATED MANSIONS IN STAFFORDSHIRE

BLITHFIELD HALL

SK 044239

Ralph Bagot married the heiress of the manor of Blithfield in the mid 14th century, and in the 1390s Sir John Bagot constructed a new moated mansion. It may have been of timber as in 1398 he sued the carpenter Robert Stanlowe for 40 marks for faulty work. The existing hall has a late 16th century west range but is mostly of 1740 and 1822, and the moat has long since disappeared.
See: Pevsner p72-3; Greenslade & Stuart p22-3; Country Life

CHILLINGTON HALL

SJ 864068

The curved stretch of water surviving in 1756 was probably a relic of a moat which may have dated from the Giffard family's original association with the manor in the 12th century. Sir John Giffard, d1556, built a new house of which the inner courtyard remains, but most of the present facades and rooms are of the early and later 18th century, with the saloon corresponding to the medieval hall.
See: Larkham T.S.S.A.H.S. XXIV p37; Pevsner p102-4

COPPENHALL GORSE MOAT

SJ 906203

The large overgrown oval platform is now again surrounded by water which is of considerable width on the SE side. Excavation in 1951 suggested the site was occupied in the 14th century.
See: V.C.H. Staffs I p362

HAMSTALL HALL

SK 105194

Hardly any traces now remain of the de Ridwares' moated mansion by the west bank of the River Blythe south of the bridge.

A comparatively small but imposing brick tower north of the churchyard was the status symbol and lookout tower of a quadrangular mansion built by the Coton family in c1500. Later in the 16th century the Fitzherberts enlarged the hall and the tower was then adapted to serve as a stair turret. Most of the mansion, which was probably moated, was demolished in the 18th century, but the tower was allowed to remain, although derelict, as a folly, or eye catcher. A brick gatehouse with a pair of low octagonal turrets remains to the north.
See: T.S.S.A.H.S. XXIV p42 & XXVI

The brick lookout tower at Hamstall Ridware.

Himley Hall as it was in 1735 (reproduced by courtesy of E.P.Publishing)

HANDSACRE HALL

SK 090156

Three dry arms of the moat survive beside a new housing estate. A drawbridge remained until the early 18th century, and Shaw in 1798 reports that the derelict timber mansion then standing within bore the year 1663 on a beam, which is probably when it was rebuilt.
See: Shaw p210-11; Larkham - S.S.A.H.S. XXIV 1982-3 p35

HIMLEY HALL

SO 888916

The present mid 18th century hall with extensions of 1824-7 lies on the site of a late medieval moated mansion of brick and stone shown still intact in an engraving of 1735 published in Shaw's book of 1798. The wet moat may have dated back to the time of William Beresford, owner in c1316 under the overlordship of the de Somery family of Dudley, but the picture suggests that much of the house was built for the Sutton lords of Dudley at the turn of the 15th and 16th centuries. Lord Dudley and Ward built the present Hall.

LAPLEY MANOR

SJ 873130

There are slight remains of the ditch which surrounded the precinct of Lapley Priory. After the Priory was dissolved at the beginning of the 15th century a manor house was built on the site of the conventual buildings to the north of the church. This was walled and probably moated, and in 1643 held a Parliamentary garrison of 70 men. In December of that year Colonel Heveningham captured the house for the King by scaling the walls with ladders. Most of the wall was demolished soon after and is not shown on a drawing made in c1800, although some of it then still survived.
See: V.C.H.Staffs I p364; IV p144

LITTYWOOD MOAT

SJ 889190

The surname de la Motte is associated with this site in 1175. The innermost of two circular concentric moats is earlier than the centrally placed timber framed hall with brick infilling built in c1400 for the de Caverswall family. The wide inner moat is dry but for a small pool, and surrounds a platform roughly 35m square. The outer moat is about one fifth water filled, and encloses an area about 160m in diameter.
See: V.C.H. Staffs I p359; T.S.S.A.H.S. XXIV p36; Pevsner p76

MOAT HOUSE, TAMWORTH

SK 202039

This mansion was built in the 1570s by the Comberford family, and lies off Lichfield Street, west of the castle. It has traces of its former wet moat fed from the adjacent River Teme.
See: T.S.S.A.H.S. XXIV p48; Pevsner p278-9

MAVESYN RIDWARE HALL

SK 081168

Nothing remains of the moat which once surrounded the mansion. The gatehouse range of a quadrangular building set around a courtyard still survives in front of a house built in 1718. The range dates from the 14th century, and is timber framed except for the outer wall, which is of stone with a brick upper part probably of 1718. The house was built by the Mavesyns and passed to the Cawardens in 1403 when Sir Robert Mavesyn was slain at the battle of Shrewsbury.
See: T.S.S.A.H.S. XXIV p44; Pevsner p203-4

The remains of Norbury Manor.

Norbury Manor as it was in c1686.

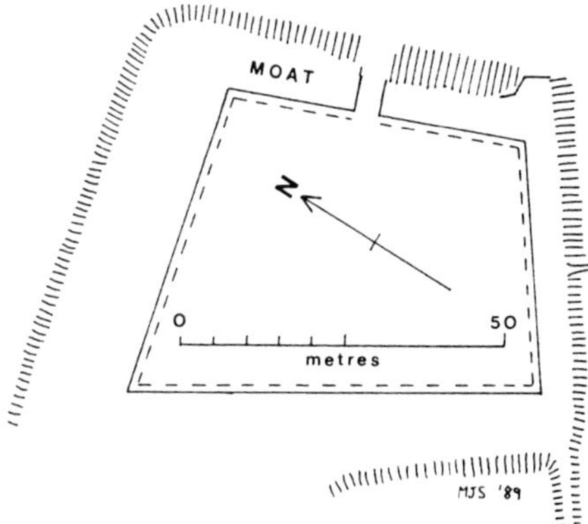

PLAN OF NORBURY MANOR

NORBURY MANOR SJ 797233

According to Stebbing Shaw the moated mansion was built by the elder Ralph Butler, lord of the manor from c1291 to 1307. In 1521 the Butlers sold the manor to Thomas Skrymsher, d1551, a prothonotary of the Court of Common Pleas. The Skrymshers in turn sold Norbury to George Anson of Shugborough in 1775. By 1801 the manor house was in a state of decay, and was only inhabited by farmworkers, and in 1838 it was demolished, a new house being built to the south.

Although the old mansion is thus lost its platform has still survived intact. It is an irregularly shaped quadrangle with sides about 64, 38, 47, and 48 metres long respectively, and has retaining walls of good sandstone ashlar about a metre thick, which was also probably the thickness of the walling above. The moat is now nearly dry. It was of variable width, and widened into a pool at the west corner where a stream leads into it.

Luckily, a drawing of the house as it was in c1686 survives. It shows the entrance front which faced NE. The gateway is positioned in the middle and appears to have then been reached by a bridge, although there is now a causeway on its site. The lower part of the walling shown could well be of c1300 but the upper two levels of mullion and transom windows with gables above to the south of the gateway, and the jettied gallery to the north, must have been 16th century, while the east corner bartizan was probably late medieval.
See: V.C.H. Staffs IV p155-6

OKEOVER HALL SK 158482

The moat shown around the house in Plot's view of 1686 could have dated back as far as the Sir Hugh de Okeover of 1180-1212. A need for defence was demonstrated in 1449 when the Cockayne brothers of Ashbourne raided Okeover whilst Phillip de Okeover was in London. They seriously damaged the house and killed all but five of the deer. The moat was probably filled for the new work of the 1740s.
See: article in Country Life magazine.

Pillaton Hall

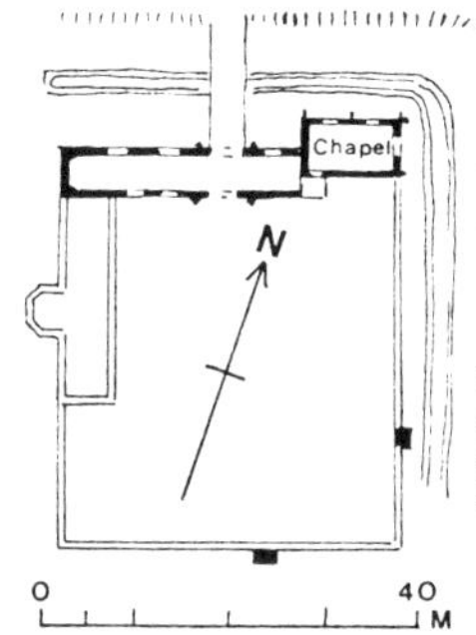

PLAN OF
PILLATON HALL

PILLATON OLD HALL

SJ 943129

The manor of Pillaton was held by Burton Abbey, and then in 1546 was granted to Sir William Paget, whose descendants held it until the 18th century. However, Pillaton Hall, to the SE of Penkridge, was occupied by the Littleton family from at least the early 16th century, and the chapel, at least, is probably slightly older than that. In 1754 the moated house was taxed on no less than 25 hearths and Lady Littleton was in residence. Sir Edward Littleton, 1st Lord Hatherton, moved further north to Teddesley, away from the mining around Cannock. In 1786 only a farmer lived at Pillaton, and the chapel was ruinous. The demolition then described as imminent had taken place by 1800 when a drawing shows only the north range and eight tall chimney stacks from the other ranges, which for some unknown reason were left standing. Several of these fell by 1841, when Buckley made some drawings of the house, but in 1884-8 the surviving range was repaired by Lord Hatherton.

The narrow brick built north range has in the middle a gateway with four centered arches and turrets, although the latter may be of the rebuild of the upper parts carried out in 1706. East of the gate is the stone chapel of St Modwena, with typical 15th century windows. The hall lay in the south range and the solar was on the east, and the kitchen lay in the west range. A new range has just been constructed on this side for the present owners to augment the limited accommodation available west of the gateway. The moat was drained in c1860, but narrow ornamental pools have now been laid out along the north and east sides.

See V.C.H. Staffs V p119-120

PRESTWOOD MOAT

SJ 946018

Prestwood is a corruption of Priest wood and was held by the Dean and chapter of the college at Wolverhampton. However, they probably sub-let it, as in the late 13th century Henry, son of William de Essex, made "a certain watery place in the wood of Prestwood". The old house, by then a farm, was burnt in 1612, and its successor was built to the west. Part of the moat survived until 1972.

See: T.S.S.A.H.S. XXIV p41

RED MOOR MOAT SK 043117

This rectangular earthwork 100m long by 70m wide lying in woodland beside a stream is probably the place that Henry II visited in 1155 after aquiring a small Cistercian abbey whose occupants had moved to Warwickshire. Money was spent on it in 1157 and 1162. The ditch is now almost dry.
See: T.S.S.A.H.S. XXIV p38

SHARESHILL MOAT SJ 946067

A school playground now lies on the site of this mansion. The site was long thought to be Roman, but excavations showed that it began in the 12th century with a timber revetted ditch and bank around timber buildings. In the 13th century it was given a wider ditch with a sandstone retaining wall on the inner side. Subsequently these defences were levelled and new timber buildings set on stone footings, and probably comprising a chapel, hall and tower, and a dwelling chamber, were built, only to be abandoned by c1400.
See: T.S.S.A.H.S. XXIV p46-7

SHENSTONE PARK MOAT SK 119035

The well preserved water filled moat near the farm may be a relic of a hunting lodge first established in the late 11th century by the D'Oyley family. Henry III licensed a park here in 1236. Some recent excavations produced little of interest.
See: T.S.S.A.H.S. XXIV p47

SINAI PARK SK 223231

On a hill overlooking Burton on trent is a derelict timber framed and brick house of c1500 which may have been a summer house of the Abbots of Burton Abbey. The wet moat around it has been recently re-dug but the house itself still awaits restoration.
See: Pevsner p77; V.C.H. Staffs I p358

WYCHNOR MOAT SK 175159

Beside the canal to the south of the church are three dry arms of the moat of what was described in Henry VIII's reign as a ruinous old mansion subject to flooding.
See: T.S.S.A.H.S. XXIV p58

CASTLES IN THE WEST MIDLANDS COUNTY

BESCOT HALL

SP 998967

This mansion stood in what is now Pleck Park between the entrance from Bescot Drive and the M6, immediately north of junction 9. The last traces of the moats, which were double on the NW side, finally disappeared in c1970. In 1271 William Hillary held land in Bescot, and was granted a considerable amount more in c1300 by his overlord Roger de Morteyn, Lord of Walsall. The moats were probably dug in that era, and in 1311 William Hillary was besieged there by fifty men led by Thomas le Rous. In 1345 William's son Sir Roger Hillary was given a licence to crenellate by Edward III. In the early 15th century Bescot passed to the Mountford family. Sir Simon Mountford was attainted of treason in 1495, but the family recovered Bescot in 1534, and held it until the 1670s. It was then a dwelling of considerable substance, being taxed on 14 hearths in 1666.

Bescot later passed to the Slaneys and several other families. In the 18th century the old hall was demolished and replaced by a new house NE of the moat, over which a bridge was built. The new hall was enlarged in the 1790s, but was leased to tenants by the mid 19th century, and was in turn demolished in c1930.

See: V.C.H. Warwickshire VII p171-2

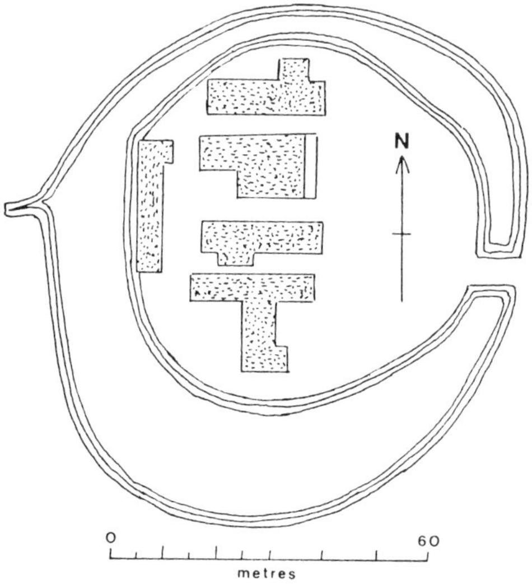

BIRMINGHAM MOAT

SP 074865

The manor of Birmingham was long held by a family of knights who took their name from the place, which they held under a series of overlords. In 1166 Peter de Birmingham, son of William, Steward of Dudley, was authorised to hold a market at his castle of Birmingham. After William de Birmingham was killed fighting on the de Montfort side at the battle of Evesham in 1265 he was disinherited and Roger de Clifford had possession for a while, but a later William de Birmingham recovered the manor in c1302. A year before his death in 1425 the ninth William de Birmingham was ejected from the manor by Sir Edmund Ferrers during a dispute over ownership of it.

Edward Birmingham was the last resident lord of the manor. He got into debt as a result of insufficient supervision while still a minor, was convicted of a felony, and in 1536 surrendered the manor to Henry VIII in return for a pension. In 1557 the manor was granted to Thomas Marrow, whose descendents sold it in 1746 to the Archer family. However, these families let the property and a new house was built in c1740 for the manufacturer John Francis, although some medieval outbuildings then still survived.

The buildings had all gone by 1816, when the moat was filled in and the Smithfield Market built on the site. This in turn was demolished in 1959, and the opportunity was taken to excavate part of the site before redevelopment. Footings of an ashlar faced wall of a hall or range of apartments were found on the western part of the site. Dating evidence was inconclusive, but the middle third of the 13th century, or the early 14th, are the most likely periods for its construction. Hanson's 1778 plan of Birmingham shows five separate structures standing in the western half of a platform with an average diameter of about 65m. The moat was about 10m wide on the north and east, but wider on the other sides. The site lies on the southern half of the quadrangle now enclosed by Jamaica Row, Moat Row, Moat Lane, and St Martin's Lane, being only 100m SE of St Martin's Church. Hanson also shows a wet moat about 8m wide around a platform roughly 30m in diameter on which stood the parsonage. This lay across what it now the north end of Pershore St, close to where it joins Edgbaston St, some 200m SW of St Martin's Church. *See: V.C.H. Warwickshire VII; T.B.A.S. 89, 1978-9*

Caludon Castle.

CALUDON CASTLE

SP 374802

At the end of the 12th century the Earl of Chester granted Caludon to Stephen de Segrave, who probably built the first manor house. A park of 20 acres and a pool are recorded at Caludon in 1279 and Edward I licensed John de Segrave to crenellate the manor house in 1305. On the death of John, Lord Segrave in 1353 Caludon passed to his daughter Elizabeth and her husband John de Mowbray, who are thought to have obtained another licence for crenellation in 1354. In 1385 a tiled building of four bays inside the bridge, a tiled building of seven bays outside the bridge, and a thatched barn of five bays are recorded as being in a poor state of repair. Thomas Mowbray was created Duke of Norfolk in 1397, and was residing at Caludon in 1398 when he appeared at Gosford Green for the abortive duel which Richard II had ordered him to fight with the Duke of Hereford after each had accused the other of treason. In the event the King stopped the fight before it began and banished both.

After the death of the Lady Anne Mowbray, wife of Richard, Duke of York, in 1481, the castle passed to William, Lord Berkeley, and Henry, Lord berkeley is said to have rebuilt it in the 1580s, with further additions being made by Elizabeth, Lady Berkeley in the early 17th century. In 1631 George, Lord Berkeley sold Caludon to Thomas Morgan, in whose time, or shortly after, the place was left to decay, possibly as a result of damage received during or after a supposed siege in the Civil War. The lands passed through the Preston and Clifford families before being broken up in 1815. Just over a century later Coventry Corporation aquired most of the land for housing, but the castle site was luckily preserved as a public recreation ground.

The site now comprises a level platform 70m long by 48m wide surrounded, except on the east, where it has been filled in, by a ditch about 15m wide which is now dry. This platform may date from the time of the 1305 licence but the one fragment of masonry still standing within it about 5m away from the north side, has windows of a form which must be later, and fit much better with the date of the supposed second licence of 1354. The fragment is 2m thick and 10m high by 12.5m long and represents two complete bays, with the ends of two other bays, of the north wall of a block containing the main castle hall set over a basement. There are remains of two light windows at both levels, the hall windows having ogival heads and being large and impressive.

See: V.C.H. Warwickshire VIII p121

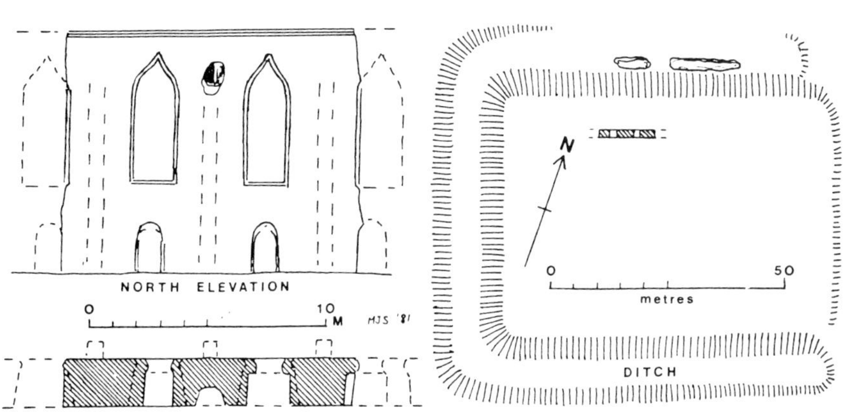

PLANS OF CALUDON CASTLE

Castle Bromwich Motte.

CASTLE BROMWICH MOTTE

SP 143901

This mound lies north of Castle Bromwich church overlooking the River Tame and junction 5 on the M6. One of the feeder roads for the latter has been cut through the site of the large bailey to the east and south, leaving the mound curiously isolated with a high retaining wall on its south side, while the northern side has suffered from natural subsidence. The mound is now only about 5m high, but would have appeared higher when the ditch separating it from the bailey existed on the sides facing flat ground. Nothing now remains of a monument erected on it in the 19th century by the Bridgmans. Castle Bromwich was held in the 12th and 13th centuries by a family of knights called de Bromwich with the Paganels and de Someries of Dudley as their overlords.
See: V.C.H. Warwickshire IV p44

COVENTRY CASTLE & CITY WALLS

SP 336788

At about the time of William II's accession in 1087, Coventry was given to the Earl of Chester. He or one of his early 12th century successors built a castle there. In 1143 Robert Marmion of Tamworth seized the adjacent priory, and fortified it against the Earl, and in 1146 King Stephen ordered the castle to be surrendered to him. The Earl tried to recover the castle by force in 1147, but Stephen came to relieve it. There were several skirmishes in the neighbourhood, during which the King was slightly wounded but succeeded in routing the earl. The King then demolished the castle, but it was evidently rebuilt as it is referred to in charters of the reigns of Henry II and John. However, Earl Ranulph de Blundeville, d1232, seems to have abandoned the castle in favour of greater seclusion at the manor house of Cheylesmore further to the south (see page 60).
See: V.C.H. Warwickshire VIII p118

Swanswell Gate, Coventry City Walls.

Coventry's size and importance must have caused it to have a ditch and other rudimentary defences by the late 12th century. In 1329 Edward III granted the priory and citizens a licence for the building of embattled walls around the city but work only appears to have begun in 1335, when the mayor, Richard de Stoke, laid the first stone of New Gate. Work proceeded slowly around the south and west sides throughout the later 14th century and then in the 15th the priory lands north of the Sherborne were enclosed. The work was only just finished before Leland's visit in the 1530s as the city found the construction and maintenance of the walls a considerable financial burden. The defences were sufficient, however, to enable the city to play a part as a fortress in the struggles of the 1450s and 60s. By the early 17th century the walls were already becoming neglected but were restored by pro-Parliamentarian forces in 1642. In that year King Charles I appeared before the city and breached New Gate with cannonfire before Lord Brooke arrived and the King withdrew to the north, leaving Brooke to set up his headquarters in the city. A tower was built, and other work carried out on the walls in 1644 in readiness for a Royalist siege which never took place.

Charles II saw Coventry as a den of rebels and in 1662 sent the Earl of Northampton to demolish its walls. Only part was destroyed before there was a change of heart, the remainder being maintained in the 1670s and 80s, with several gatehouses being let as private dwellings. All twelve gates survived well into the 18th century and were only demolished when they began to hinder traffic.

The walls at Coventry were nearly three miles long, enclosing an area three quarters of a mile long by half a mile wide, which was equalled only at London and Norwich. All that survives is a ruinous length connecting the simple rectangular Cook Street Gate and Swanswell Gate, being within a park called Lady Herbert's Garden. New Gate, removed in 1762, was rectangular with a single turret, later replaced by two gables. Gosford Gate, removed in 1765, had round bartizans on the outer side and adjoined St George's chapel. Spon Gate, demolished in 1771, had two polygonal towers on the outer side, and the inner side of the lowest level extended almost to St John's church. The Greyfriars Gate was built soon after the additional licence granted in 1385, and was demolished in 1781. It was rectangular with two round towers on the outer corners. Bishop Street Gate was built by 1411, rebuilt in 1689, and taken down in 1765. It was a two storey rectangular structure. Well Street Gate, Hill Street Gate, and Bastille Gate were all similar. The latter was given an extra storey in the late 17th century, and survived until 1849, being the last of the gates to be destroyed.
See: V.C.H. Warwickshire VIII p21-4

DUDLEY CASTLE

SO 946907

William the Conqueror gave extensive estates centered on Dudley to William FitzAnsculph in c1071. The Domesday survey of 1086 states that "the said William holds Dudley and there is his castle", so the earthworks evidently existed by then. Early in the 12th century a large part of FitzAnsculph's estate, including Dudley, passed to Fulke Paganel, probably by marriage. Fulke's son Ralph supported the Empress Matilda against King Stephen. In 1138 the latter came to Dudley and laid the district waste, although the castle appears to have been untaken. However, in 1175 it was destroyed by Henry II because Ralph's son Gervase had supported the King's sons in their rebellion of 1174. Gervase later paid 500 marks to regain his lands and the King's favour, and at his death in 1194 was succeeded by his sister's son Ralph de Somery. At that time the castle seems to have only ranked as an unfortified house, if it was used at all.

In c1261 Roger de Somery began to fortify his manor house at Dudley, but Henry III prevented this until 1264, when, having gained royal favour for his support of the king against the rebel barons, he was licensed to make the manor house into a castle with a ditch and a wall of stone and lime. The bailey wall may thus have been constructed by him or his son Roger, who succeeded in 1282, but it is fairly certain that the keep on the mound was built in the troubled reign of Edward II by John de Somery, who succeeded as a minor in 1291, was knighted in 1306, and lived until 1321. William de Beresford and other neighbours complained of John 'that he has obtained such mastery in the county of Stafford that no man can obtain law or justice therein; that he has made himself more than a king there; that no one can dwell there unless he buys protection from him either by money or assisting him in building his castles, and that he attacks people in their own houses with the intention of killing them unless they make fine for his protection".

On John de Somery's death Dudley went to his sister Margaret, wife of John de Sutton. The latter became heavily in debt to John de Charlton, who was in possession of Dudley in 1329-30, probably on the strength of the debt, when it was besieged by a number of local notables. In c1340-60 the Suttons built a new hall and the block containing the principal private apartments and chapel.

Dudley Castle: The northern domestic apartments.

The sixth successive John de Sutton served Henry VI as a Lord Lieutenant of Ireland. He was wounded at the battle of St Albans and for a short while incarcerated by Edward IV in the Tower of London. His grandson was the Edmund Dudley who did so much to build up Henry VII's fortune, and was rather ungratefully executed by the King who spent the money, Henry VIII, in 1510. Edmund's son John, however, rose high in the royal favour, becoming Viscount Lisle in 1542, Earl of Warwick in 1547, and then Duke of Northumberland. He obtained Dudley in c1533, and remodelled the hall and built a fine new set of apartments to the north of it, and probably also the outer bailey walls. Queen Mary executed him in 1553 after he made an abortive attempt to have Lady Jane Grey, married to his son Guildford, crowned as Queen. In 1554 Dudley was granted to Edward Dudley, a kinsman, who in 1575 entertained Queen Elizabeth at the castle. In the 1580s Dudley Castle was surveyed as a possible place of confinement for Mary, Queen of Scots but was never used as such.

On the death of the last of the male line of the Sutton Dudleys in 1643 the castle passed to the Ward family. It was held for the King by Thomas Leveson in 1643, and in 1644 withstood a siege by the Earl of Denbigh. It was surrendered eventually in 1646 to Sir William Brereton without a siege, and in 1647 was made untenable as a fortress by demolishing the outer half of the keep, and barbican, and making breaches in the bailey walls. The castle remained in use as a residence, and in the 1690s Edward Ward, Lord Dudley, built a new block of apartments between the keep and gatehouse, but in 1750 the habitable parts were accidentally destroyed by fire and the Ward family then transferred to Himley Hall.

Dudley Castle lies 200m up on a limestone ridge high above the town. It has an oval bailey about 100m from north to south by 80m wide, with on the SW a mound rising a further 9m. The surrounding ditch on the north side is now used for zoological purposes, and beyond it is an outer platform. Another outer platform on the south has thin 16th century curtain walls with a rectangular gatehouse and a round corner tower.

The main castle courtyard was surrounded by a wall 2m thick in the late 13th or early 14th century. The wall has been heightened on the eastern side, where the domestic apartments are against it. On the north side it has been replaced by thinner 16th century walling with an unfortified secondary gateway. On the west side, and on either side of the gateway, gaps were made at the slighting of 1647. The square gatehouse, which may incorporate some late 12th century masonry in the side walls, is contemporary with the wall and originally only projected inside it. However, the two storey lodgings built in the 1690s on the west side, and the new walling on the east side, were built flush with the inner wall of the gate-house. The inner and outer gateway arches have portcullis grooves. In front of the gateway is a barbican, which here took the form of an open porch with two round corner towers, now destroyed down to their bases. The wall between the towers is a later insertion.

The hall is a splendid chamber nearly 24m long by 9.5m wide. It lies above cellars and is mostly the work of Sir William Sharington for the Duke of Northumberland in c1550, with some older masonry. A central set of steps led up to a loggia added in front of the hall. At the south end of the loggia was a staircase and at the north end is a porch giving onto the service end of the hall which was probably screened off with a musicians' gallery set above. North of the hall are a pair of 16th century ranges, the nearest having a bow window, and the furthest an octagonal stair turret near the north gateway. Both ranges contained service rooms at ground level, two storeys of fine apartments above, with large windows towards the court, and on top were attics in the roofs, which have gables towards the court. South of the hall is a large mid 14th century block with the solar and chapel set side by side over cellars.

Dudley Castle: The Mound and Keep from the South.

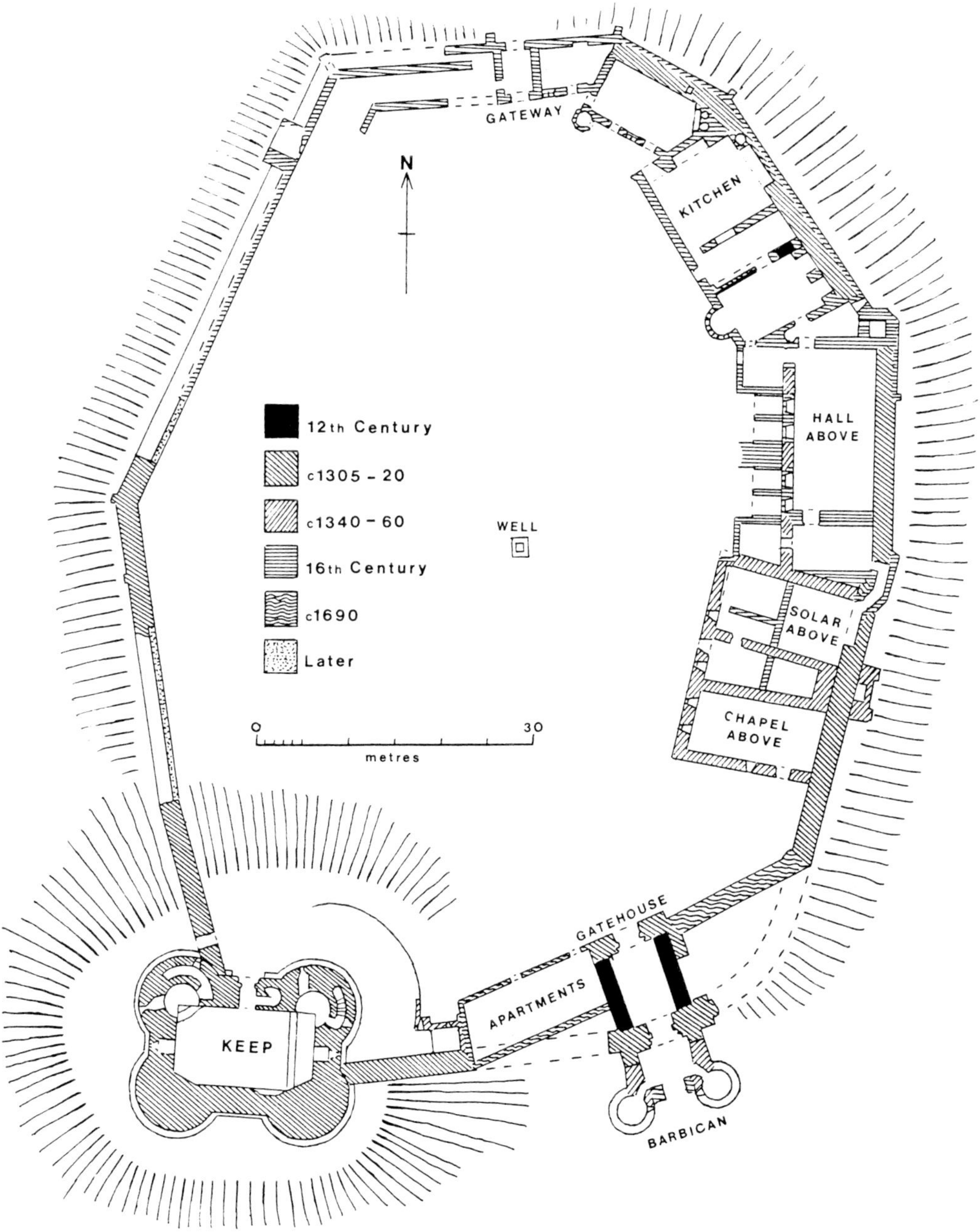

PLAN OF DUDLEY CASTLE

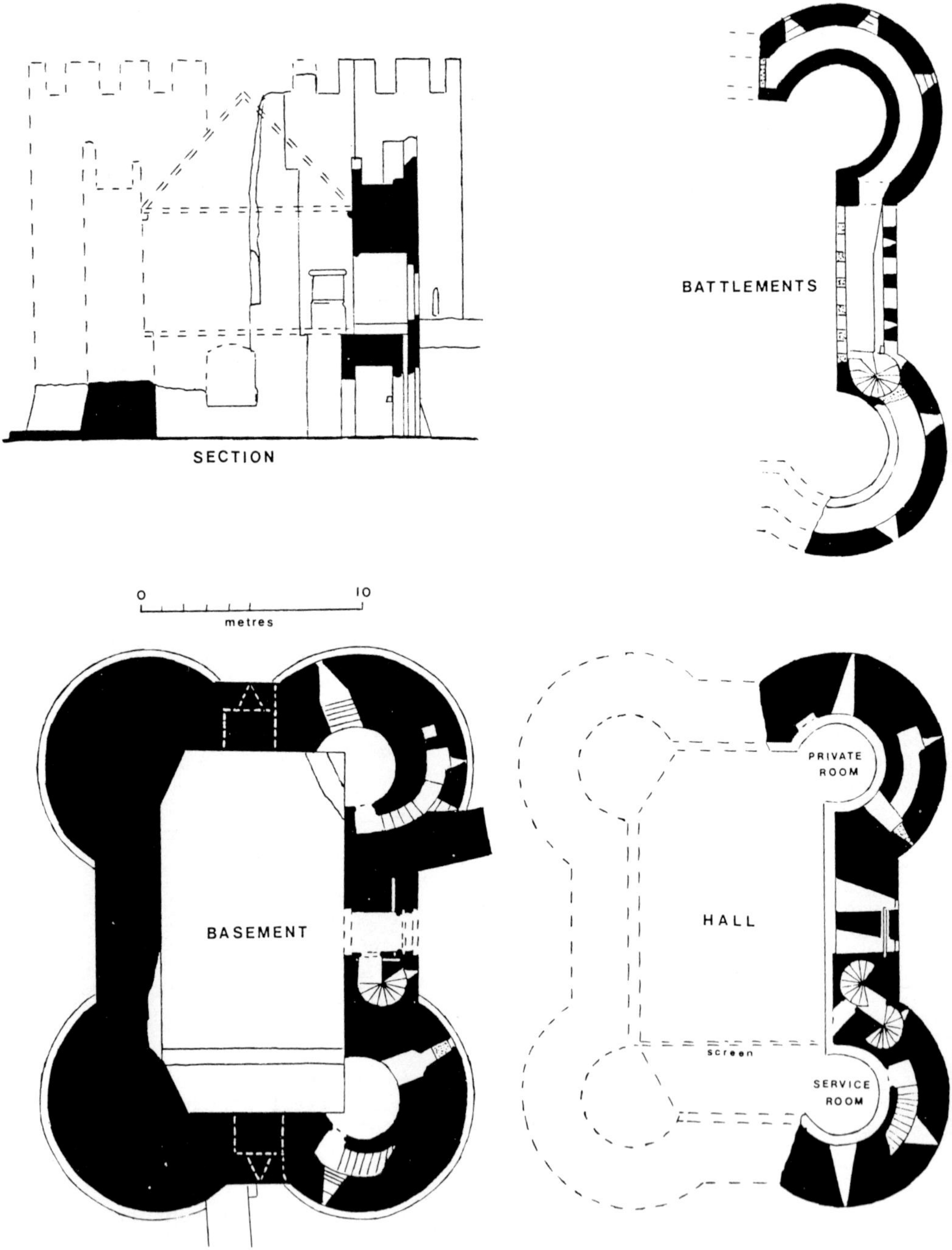

PLANS & SECTION OF THE KEEP OF DUDLEY CASTLE

Between the mound summit and the lodgings west of the gateway is a pit which evidently formed part of the 14th century access to the keep. Originally there would have been stairs here leading to a doorway closed by a drawbridge set in a turret on the line of a low embattled wall around the edge of the mound summit. The tower house or keep set within this court is still imposing and of great interest despite the southern, or outermost, part of it having been destroyed to within 2m of the ground in 1647. The tower house is 21.8m long by 14.8m wide externally, and has a circular tower 9.8m in external diameter projecting slightly from each corner. At the lowest level the southern towers were solid and the main walls are 3m thick except for the thicker north wall containing the entrance. This was closed by a portcullis operated from two narrow embrasures with windows lighting the hall above. From the eastern side of the entrance rises a spiral stair to the east end of the hall, which was evidently screened off. At hall level the NE drum contained a service room with a secondary stair down for conveying food and drink. The NW tower contains a fireplace and a latrine, and must have been partitioned off as a private room, while other chambers suitable for sleeping in were probably provided in the southern drums. From the top of the main stair a second spiral stair leads to the wallwalk 11m above ground. The towers contained galleries at this level to allow all round access to the other sections of the wallwalk. They were evidently roofed over at the same level as the hall, without habitable spaces above. However their walls rose one more level to higher battlements with merlons reaching 16m high above the ground. These merlons were either unusable dummies or had wooden fighting platforms reached by wooden ladders. The keep thus formed a private and secure, but rather cramped, residence. Later owners probably preferred the more spacious rooms in the bailey.

See: Archaeological Journal LXXXI pp1-24

Dudley Castle: Chapel South window.

LANGLEY CASTLE SP 152956

In 1327 Edmund de Barford was licensed to crenellate his house at Langley. That he may well have considered himself in need of some protection is demonstrated by the events of the previous generation when his father William complained about the depredations of John de Somery of Dudley castle. Langley was later held by the Pudseys. Traces of footings of possible 14th century stonework and slight remains of later brick walls were visible earlier this century but all that now remains are two tree covered depressions marking the line of two sections of the moat. The other side of the moat was filled in early in this century. By the site is a newly renovated stable block of much later date, now to be used as housing.

See: T.B.A.S. 1947-8 Vol LXVII

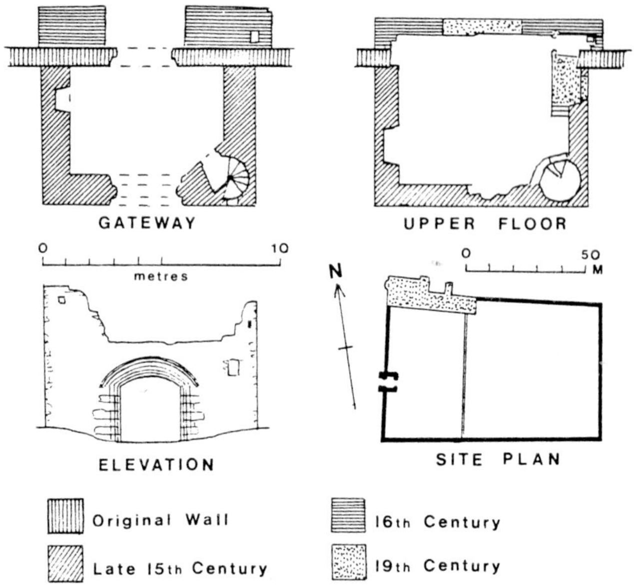

PLANS OF RUSHALL HALL

RUSHALL HALL

SP 026998

Rushall formed part of the barony of Dudley until 1322, but from at least the 1160s was held by the Rushall family until the 1230s, when it passed to the Boweles family. The date of the thin but high curtain walls is uncertain. The men working for William de Boweles whose tools were confiscated by officials of Cannock Forest in 1292 could have been illegally quarrying limestone for the walls. That they were needed is shown by the incident in 1323 when a notorious local trouble-maker, John de Wetales, attacked the house of William de Boweles at Rushall because he gave refuge to Robert de Eslinton. John was said to have shot arrows over the gate and was later fined.

However, the walls may be of c1400 when 'Geffrey Ive pulled doun an olde halle at Rushale, and set up a newe hall' when his daughter became the second wife of William Grobbere. About 30 years later their daughter Eleanor brought Rushall to John Harpur. Later in the 15th century the Harpurs added the gatehouse on the western side of the enclosure, whilst the Leighs, who obtained the manor in 1540, added a third storey at the end of the 16th century.

Edward Leigh supported Parliament in the Civil War, and in 1643 Rushall Hall was besieged and captured in his absence by the Royalists under Prince Rupert, Lady Leigh with 'only helpe of her men and maides' having valiantly defended her house'. In May 1644 the hall was besieged and captured by the Earl of Denbigh, although he described it as 'watered round about, admirable works where are four forts at each end of the house one, from the water to the top of the works is some four or five yards high, besides the breadth of the trench, which is answerable to it, and a stone wall within the works much higher, besides a very strong drawbridge, and but only one passage through the stone wall into the house, which is as strong as art can make it, and within the wall, in the yard, they have made galleries for their better defence, and greate stones laid thick round the works, which upon any assault would have done as much execution as the muskets".

The hall passed by marriage from the Leighs to the Mellishes in 1811. They occupied the house for a while and the gatehouse upper rooms were then still fit to take guests, but by 1845 the place had been let to a farmer who took down the upper part of the gatehouse and part of the curtain wall, and burnt the stone to obtain lime. However, what remained of the gate and wall found better treatment when the antiquarian W.H.Duignan lived at the hall in 1857-1889.

The curtain wall enclosed a court 90m long by 56m wide and is some 6.3m high in places, but is only 0.7m thick and was without a wallwalk. No crenellations or any towers or turrets, other than the gatehouse, have survived, and there probably never were any, although there was a moat. The considerable earthworks raised in the Civil war to make the place defensible against the techniques and weapons then used in sieges have left scarcely any traces.

The gatehouse was built over the original simple arch through the wall, which in its present form looks early 15th century. The building is just over 9m wide, and projects 6m into the court. A spiral stair in the NE corner leads to the room above the gateway. The part of the gateway which projects outside the walls was added slightly later. It has a crude archway with above it a stone with the Harpur arms. The upper rooms as remodelled had mullion and transom windows, as shown on old drawings. The gateway at one time formed part of a range of offices and outbuildings.

The present dwelling in the NW corner of the court contains a little ancient work, but the original main apartments are likely to have been laid out from north to south across the enclosed area creating two separate courtyards.

See: T.S.S.A.H.S. 1981-2 XXIII p79-88

WALSALL MANOR

SP 001984

The first house on this site may have been built in King John's reign, when William le Rous created a park in this area. The moat which survived until recently, however, was dug either in 1338-9 when the two manors of Walsall were reunited in the hands of Ralph Lord Basset, d1343, or in the mid 1380s when there is a mention of 543 cartloads of stone for a castle which Sir Ralph Basset was intending to build in support of his kinsman the Earl of Warwick against Richard II. This, however, was not built, or at least not in its intended form, although in 1388-9 a moated mansion here was given a new drawbridge, and a latrine, and the wooden gates were plated with iron, and further maintenance was carried out in 1396.

Under a settlement of 1339 Walsall passed in 1390 on Sir Ralph Basset's death to Thomas Beauchamp, Earl of Warwick. As there was no resident lord the manor house was abandoned in the early 15th century, and in 1438-9 the moat is recorded as leased as a fishery. The house disappeared by 1576, and in c1870 the northern part of the moat was filled in and built upon. The rest of the moat still contained water until the 1970s, when it was mostly filled, leaving only a shallow depression around the flats then built within it as adjuncts to the nearby hospital. Excavations in 1973-4 found that the original manor house was undefended and appeared to have been let out for metal working before being later reconstructed as a moated residence.

See: V.C.H. Staffs. T.S.S.A.H.S. 1974-5 XVI p19-53

WEOLEY CASTLE

SP 022827

Weoley belonged to William FitsAnsculf, Lord of Dudley, when the Domesday Survey was made in 1086. It passed through his daughter to the Paganels, who built the first series of timber buildings on a moated platform rather smaller than the present one. Late in the 12th century the manor passed to Roger de Somery, and either he or his son Ralph appear to have built a stone hall on the eastern part of the site. Ralph's son Roger was in 1267 licensed by Henry III to build stone walls and fortifications, and the present walls and towers are thought to have been built in the 1270s, the enclosed area extending further west than the original platform did. Later in this period a new stone hall and stone barn were added.

When Sir John de Somery died in 1322 Weoley went to his sister Joan, married to Thomas Botetort. They and their successors built another barn, the chapel, and the garderobe system in the NE corner. In 1384 the heiress Joyce de Botetort brought Weoley to Sir Hugh de Burnell, who held it until 1430, and probably built a structure on the west side of the court. In 1439 the manor descended to the Berkeleys, who were attainted by Henry VII in 1485 as supporters of the vanquished Richard III, and they were replaced by the Dudleys. They sold Weoley to Richard Jerveys, Sheriff of London, in 1536, and his descendants held it until the early 19th century, although the castle was ruined by the mid 17th century, and does not appear to have taken part in the Civil War.

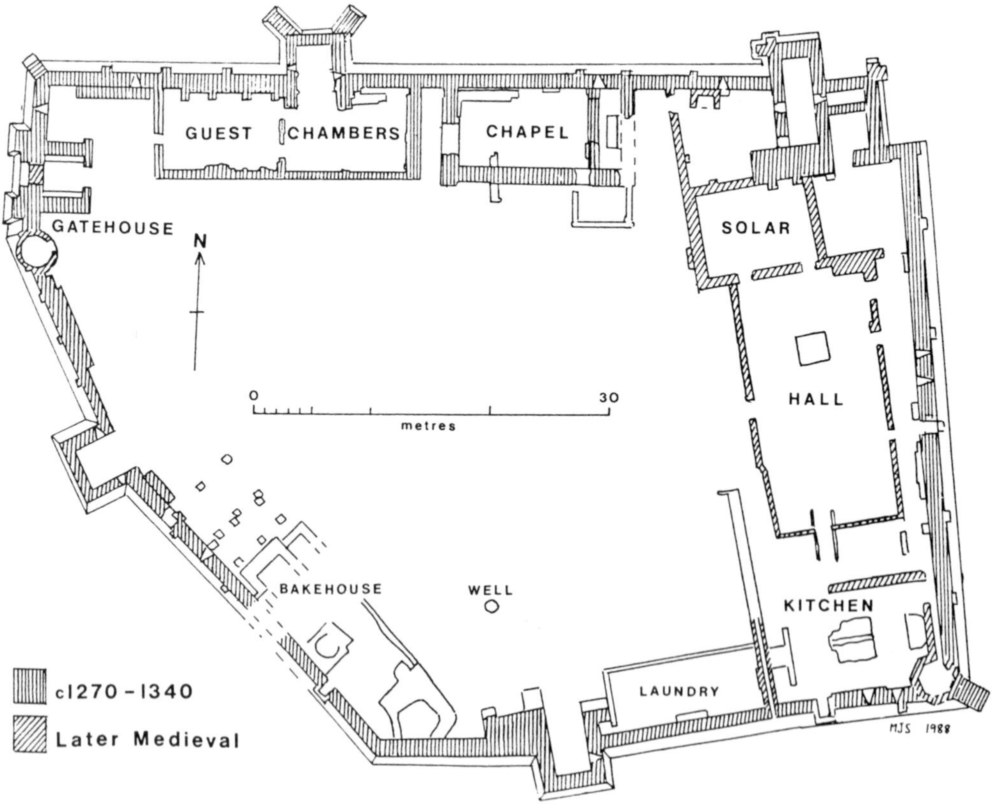

PLAN OF WEOLEY CASTLE

The N.E. corner of Weoley Castle.

The castle has a low lying site beside a stream and for defence much reliance must have been placed on a wide wet moat. By the 20th century the buildings had crumbled away almost down to courtyard level and were covered with silt and debris. Little architecturally was known of them prior to a long series of excavations started in the 1930s, and continuing up until 1962. Despite the loss of early excavation reports in a fire during the War, it has been possible to reconstruct most of the history of the site.

In plan the castle is very roughly a rectangle 75m long by 60m wide with the SW corner canted off. The surrounding wall averaged 1.2m thick above a broad battered plinth rising from the bottom of the moat, and had thin decorative pilaster buttresses at intervals. There are small square towers at the NE corner, in the middle of the north, south, and SW sides, and in the west wall near the NW corner, the latter also being the gateway until blocked up later. Before the walls existed the access to the platform was by a timber bridge on the east, and the present access by a causeway on the SW side has no precedent historically speaking.

The NE tower stands by a pit for garderobes for the solar to the south, beyond which was the later timber hall, with in the SE corner the hearths of a kitchen. The earlier stone hall remains underlie the north end of the later one and the solar block. On the SE was a small polygonal turret, perhaps of the late 14th century, and there is a second round turret corbelled out of the corner by the former gatehouse. On the north side of the court are buildings which from the detailed description of the castle made in 1424 can be deduced to be the guest apartments and chapel respectively. On the SW side are ovens and bakehouses, and between the south tower and kitchen are stone footings for a timber framed laundry block.
See: T.B.A.S. XXVIII 1902 pp51-67, 78 1962 pp61-85; Med Arch 1962/3

MOATED MANSIONS IN THE WEST MIDLANDS COUNTY

BARNHURST HALL SJ 894023

In the 16th century the house was held successively by the Leveson and Cresswell families. It was rebuilt in the early 17th century and the dovecot surviving within a new housing estate may be of about that time. Remains of the moat survived until the early 1900s. *See: T.S.S.A.H.S. 1982-3 XXIV p52*

CALDEWELLE HALL SP 035991

The surviving circular earthwork may date from the turn of the 13th and 14th centuries, when Sir Hugh de Boweles, lord of Rushall Manor, gave 'Caldewelle' to his son on the occasion of his marriage, and 'bilt and repaired a mansion, and made a moot abowte the mansion'. *See: T.S.S.A.H.S. 1982-3 XXIV p49*

CHESWICK GREEN MOAT SP 130761

Excavations were carried out on this considerable earthwork before most of it was destroyed to make way for a new housing estate. It was discovered that the defences had been created in c1300 over a previously unfortified site. The 6m wide wet moat is now filled in and only part of the 6m high and 20m wide rampart now remains. *See: V.C.H. I p399-400*

CHEYLESMORE MANOR SP 333785

In the early 13th century the Earl of Chester abandoned Coventry Castle, which was hemmed in by the fast growing city, and developed a manor house at Cheylesmore to the south. There was already an extensive park there by the 1150s. The house probably had a moat but was not seriously defensible, and Richard II demanded that it was included within the section of the city walls licensed in 1385.

From 1243 to 1329 the manor was held by the Montalts and then went to Queen Isabel, who was often in residence until her death in 1358. It then went to Edward the Black Prince, who also stayed at Cheylesmore quite often. At Richard II's accession in 1377 the manor became a royal possession, remaining so until 1549, when it was granted to John Dudley, Earl of Warwick. It was subsequently leased by the city council, and, after a lengthy dispute from 1661 with the Townsend family over possession, was sold to the city in 1706. The house was described as ruinous in c1538 and 1659, but was renovated by Sir Robert Townsend in the period 1661-85. It was later used as tenements, and parts replaced by weavers' houses.

By 1945 just two ranges remained, built of a mixture of timber brick and stone. One, probably a 14th century solar block standing at one end of the former hall in the west wing, was demolished in 1955. The surviving modest wing is partly 14th century, but the gateway through it is 16th century in its present form. *See: V.C.H. Warwickshire VIII p18-21*

DUNSTALL HALL SJ 902002

A new housing estate lies upon the site of the Courtaulds factory, for the construction of which earlier in this century the hall and its moat and gatehouse were removed. Dunstall was owned by the Hampton family until the late 15th century, and the hall is likely to have been rebuilt by Humphrey Moseley after he purchased it in 1566. The estate was later purchased in turn by the Wightwick family, the Hoskinsons, and then in 1793 by James Hordern, by whom the house was repaired and the moat preserved. *T.S.S.A.H.S. 1982-3*

PLAN OF HOBBS MOAT

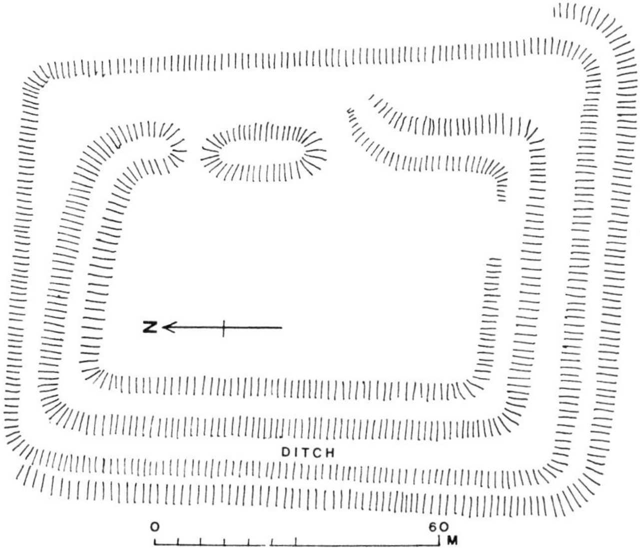

FINCHFIELD MOAT

SO 883971

The house platform and the damp depressions which were relics of three arms of the surrounding wet moat 2m deep were excavated in 1983 prior to being built upon, but nothing of interest was found. *See: T.S.S.A.H.S. XXIV p57*

HOBBS MOAT

SP 147826

This substantial earthwork lies among trees on an eminence south of Solihull. A high rampart, rising up to 6m above the dry ditch surrounding it, encloses an area 90m long by 60m wide. The site is traditionally associated with a castle or homestead belonging to the Odinsells family. It probably dates between the end of the 12th century and the beginning of the 14th century.
See: V.C.H. Warwickshire I p395

KENTS MOAT

SP 144863

This site may have been where the de Sheldon family resided in the 13th century. The de Paytos seem to have had a house here in the period 1347-73 and apparently carried out some building work, but Sir Hugh and Sir Ralph Shirley held it in the early 15th century. However there was no resident lord of the manor after 1440, and by the late 18th century all memory of buildings here were forgotten. The site was excavated in 1964 before the rampart inside the ditch was levelled and blocks of flats were built inside the enclosure.
See: V.C.H. Warwickshire I p392

NECHELLS HALL

SO 947989

Nechells Hall was a 14th century structure of two storeys. It was owned by the Hopes in the 16th century, and was taxed on 6 hearths in 1666. Its rectangular moat survived until the late 19th century. Nechells farm, which was demolished in the 1970s, had a similar moat, destroyed by mining at the turn of the century, and a smaller third moat nearby was filled up with spoil. *T.S.S.A.H.S. XXIV p55*

NEW HALL

SP 133949

The mansion within the well preserved wet moat takes its character from work done in 1870, although the south range and part of the west range have grey medieval masonry, the sandstone north range is Elizabethan, and the towers on the south and west fronts are dated 1796. The house is now used as a hotel/
See: Pevsner - Warwickshire p428.

PERRY HALL

SP 062919

The moat survives as a boating pond in a park beside the River Tame. The hall was given to John Molyneux in c1473, passed to the Fitzherberts, and then to the Smiths, who sold it in 1546 to William Stanford. The chimneys on the east side were once dated 1576, and further additions were made in 1840. It was finally demolished by Birmingham Corporation in c1929.
See: V.C.H. Warwickshire

STOWHEATH MANOR

SO 928982

The Chillington Iron Works (later Tool Co Ltd) lies on the site of a moated house probably first established in the late 13th century by Robert Burnell, Bishop of Bath and Wells, Chancellor to Edward I, as a stopping place on the way to his house at Acton Burnell in Shropshire. It was later held by the Lovells until the attainder of Francis, Lord Lovell in 1485. The moat remained complete in 1788, with a furnace close by, and was destroyed earlier this century.
See: T.S.S.A.H.S. XXIV 1982-3 p56

SYDENHAMS MOAT

SP 145757

Tipping from the 1940s onwards almost filled in the moat by 1972, when excavations were begun. The platform measured 29m by 27m and was surrounded by a wet moat 15m wide by 3m deep. It may have been built by Simon de Mancette in the early 13th century, and was sold to Sir John Dean in 1304. From 1348 until the early 17th century the manor of Monkspath in which it lies was a Montford possession, but the site was not occupied after c1400.
See: T.B.W.A.S. 1980 90 p49-64

TILEHOUSE GREEN MOAT

SP 167769

A quadrangular platform measuring 45m by 25m enclosed by a moat 18m wide was examined before a housing estate was built on it in 1983, but nothing of much interest was discovered.
See: T.B.W.A.S. 1982 92 p149-151

WEST BROMWICH OLD MANOR HOUSE

SP 005943

This house was discovered to by an important timber framed house of c1300-30 in time to be saved from demolition and renovated as a restaurant. The section of the moat in front of the Elizabethan gateway was filled in when it was built to make a forecourt, and the remainder filled in c1700, but it is now water filled again.
See: Pevsner - Staffs p303; V.C.H. Staffs XVII p17
T.S.S.A.H.S. 1975-6 p1-64

WOLVERHAMPTON OLD HALL SO 719984

The name Old Hall Street is a reminder of the large mansion built by the Levesons in c1550 in what was then open land outside the town.It had a brick walled court about 60m square with a wet moat. The hall was sold in 1715, and, with the upper storey removed, was used as a Japanning works until demolition in 1883. The moat itself survived at least until the 1830s. The Adult Education College, and the cinema and library stand on the site.
See: T.S.S.A.H.S. XXIV 1982-3 p56

OTHER EXTANT MOATS IN STAFFORDSHIRE plan on page 10)

ACTON TRUSSELL SJ 936176 Part of a circular wet moat by Manor Farm is probably a relic of the manor house of the Trussell family.

ALLEYS LANE SJ 844177 Slight traces visible of rectangular moat.

ASHMORE BROOK SK 096111 Fragment of wet moat by stream in valley.

ASTON BY STONE SJ 924316 Some remains of moat around the Hall.

BAGOT'S BROMLEY SK 066259 Some remains of moat and monument mark the site of a former house of the Bagot family.

BLAKENHALL SK 172182 Rectangular moat to the north of the Hall.

BLITHEWOOD SJ 991365 Square platform with two concentric dry moats.

BLYMHILL GRANGE SJ 811120 Well preserved dry rectangular moat.

BOODEN FARM SJ 862198 Parts of a wet moat remain around the house.

BROCKENHURST SJ 824118 Parts of two moats remain south of the farm.

BURNHILL GREEN SJ 787008 Small damaged moat behind row of houses.

CASTLECHURCH SJ 897215 Worn down dry moat west of Stafford Castle.

CHARNES OLD HALL SJ 784340 Sections of wet moat remain around hall.

COMBERFORD SK 192073 Some traces of the moat remain east of house.

COMPTON PARK FARM SO 806836 Very slight traces remain of the moat.

DOSTHILL SP 211000 Some remains of a partly wet rectangular moat.

ELFORD PARK SK 190123 Part of moat remain to north of the house of the 1760s. Part of drawbridge was dug up in late 18th century.

ESSINGTON HALL FARM SJ 951035 Rectangular moat, now partly filled.

GAYTON* SJ 978284 Most of an oval moat remains around the house.

GORSTY HILL* SK 109289 Square tree covered platform with wet moat.

HAGLEY HALL SK 042180 The large wet moat at Rugeley is probably the site of the house burnt in the 14th century and its successor.

HARLASTON SK 214110 Some slight remains to north of the church.

HARTWELL FARM SJ 917390 Some remains of the moat lie beside farm.

HILDERSTONE SJ 957347 Moated platform some way to south of hall.

HILTON SJ 952052 Two arms of wet moat lie by 18th century house.

HOLLYBUSH FARM SJ 965064 Some remains of rectangular wet moat.

HYDE FARM SJ 874078 Two arms, one wet, remain of rectangular moat.

KINGSLEY SK 007471 Some remains of large dry rectangular moat.

KNIGHTLEY DALE SJ 816237 Part of rectangular dry moat in field.

LEA MANOR SJ 749421 A moat lies to the NW of the Hall.

LITTLE ONN HALL SJ 840156 Small moat by house. Some ashlar remains.

LONGCROFT SK 150200 Some traces of moat mostly filled in the 1790s.

LUTLEY SO 816884 Rectangular moat, damaged, and ploughed down.

MAPLE HAYES SK 102101 Small, well preserved dry square moat.

MARCHINGTON WOODLANDS* SK 041296 Quadrangular wet moat in field.

MAYFIELD SK 143453 A small round wet moated enclosure on a ridge.

MOAT FARM SK 160304 There are some traces of a moat around farm.

MOAT HILL SK 136246 Part of moat remains to south of farmhouse.

MOAT HOUSE SJ 954030 Rectangular moat probably "Le Mot" mentioned in 1321. A cottage stood within it until c1930.

MOAT HOUSE BRIDGE SJ 930074 Two arms of wet moat near canal bridge.

MOAT HOUSE, LONGDON SK 077139 Slight traces of east and south arms.

NEWBOROUGH SK 076471 Rectangular moat, nearly dry, north of house.

OULTON SJ 965335 Remains of moat in field between Oulton & Garshall

PAYNSLEY HALL SJ 986380 There are remains of a moat around the hall

PENKRIDGE SJ 936135 Feint traces of three arms of moat in field.

RANTON ABBEY SJ 839244 Traces of former abbey precinct moat.

RANTON HALL SJ 847244 There are some remains of a moat around hall

RIBDEN SK 076471 Small square dry-moated platform above a house.

SANDON* SJ 956295 Wide wet moat around house, double on west side.

SHERHOLT LODGE SK 164206 Slight remains of moat beside the farm.

SIMFIELDS SJ 921469 Boggy rectangular platform. Moat very silted.

THORNTREE HOUSE SK 086303 Some traces of two rectangular platforms

TOWN HILL, YOXALL SK 143188 The damaged moat beside the bridge may go back to the 13th century, when William Ferrers, Earl of Derby gave the land to the clerk Roger de Yoxall.

WATER EATON SJ 905113 Slight traces of moat west of farm buildings.

WESTON PARK SJ 816098 rectangular moat in woods SE of the house.

WILLOUGHBRIDGE SJ 743393 Fairly well preserved rectangular dry moat.

WOODEND SK 176266 Rectangular dry moat behind the farmhouse.

WOOD HALL FARM SJ 855037 Three sides of wet moat around garden.

OTHER EXTANT MOATS IN THE WEST MIDLANDS COUNTY

ASHMOOR PARK SJ 958018 Dry rectangular moat by shopping precinct.

BERRY HALL SP 191792 A moat surrounds the fine 16th century timber framed house.

BINLEY* SP 370776 Platform with deep, partly wet, moat by school.

CALUDON SP 374799 A dry rectangular moat lies south of the castle.

CAROL GREEN SP 253777 Part of a dry moat remains around a house.

EASTCOTE HALL SP 191792 A wet moat surrounds the house, which looks Victorian but has remains of a genuine 15th century hall.

FULFORD HEATH SP 097744 Part of moat in field near Earlswood Lakes.

HEYGATE SP 053981 This rectangular dry moat near to a house may be a relic of Sir Robert Stephenson's house in the 14th century.

HOLLYBERRY END SP 265841 Part of an irregularly shaped wet moat

MERIDEN SP 242811 Slight traces of rectangular moat in field.

OVER GREEN SP 167944 A large fragmentary rectangular wet moat.

PEDDIMORE HALL* SP 154937 Rectangular wet moat around farmhouse and some remains of concentric outer moat to north and west.

PERTON COURT SO 860986 Only a fragment of the moat still remains.

SIDENHALES* SP 138751 A pool and two partly wet arms of the moat remain behind the farmhouse.

STIVICHALL* SP 317757 A square moat, now dry, but with a pool at one corner, lies by the Coventry Performing Arts Centre.

For information about numerous other former and possible moats see: V.C.H. Staffs; V.C.H.Warks; T.S.S.A.H.S. XXIV 1982-3; T.B.A.H.S.